MOTHERS ARE PEOPLE, TOO

by
Linda G. Howard

Logos International
Plainfield, New Jersey

CONTENTS

MOTHERS
ARE
PEOPLE,
TOO

Chapter 1
Mothers Are People, Too

Entering junior high school meant that Mark had to write an autobiography. I scanned his finished work. "I have two sisters . . . My father is an engineer . . . My hobbies are . . ."

The autobiography was well written but to me it had one glaring flaw. He had completely left me out. Me. And I'm his mother. I raised a disapproving eyebrow. "Well, I hope your teacher doesn't think you're a motherless child. You do have a mother, you know."

"Oh, mom," Mark said with an air of indifference, "you're only a mother. Look at Duane's mom. She's a nurse. There are plenty of things you can say about a lot of other mothers. But you're just a mother."

I steamed inside. "Mothers are people, too," I said to myself as I walked back into the kitchen to check supper.

I stirred the spaghetti as I mused, "I wonder if I mentioned my mother in my eighth grade autobiography?" I had to smile as I answered my own question. "Probably not," I thought as my self-pity melted. "She was only a mother, too."

Sometimes it seems no one else knows you are a person. You even begin to question your own self worth. With the bustle of having children, raising children and being a wife, the "you" gets lost in the shuffle. That is when self-pity and martyr complexes creep slowly, slowly into our personalities.

There is someone who does know you are a real, live person though. He is very much aware of your worth as an individual. As a wife. As a mother. His name is Jesus.

It was interesting that when the name of every great king or important man was introduced in the Old Testament his mother's name was also recorded. God knew the important role that a mother can play in any person's life. He understands the importance of molding and training a child.

Even when my children forget I'm a person, God still knows I have worth. To Him I am important. After all, even when I was a sinner, no good to anyone, He suffered the pain of the cross for me.

He is willing to take countless hours to hear me out. He is interested in the most minute details of my life. He is constantly teaching me. He wants me to enter into an abundant life with Him. In order to get me there, God is willing to take great pains and effort to show me how I should live.

Maybe to everyone, even myself, I seem unimportant, but to Jesus I am a people!

Chapter 2
Good Advice from Strange Places

Upon the birth of my first child, Mark, I became the leading child expert of the age. Armed with the fifteen page booklet given to me by my pediatrician and a telephone number where he could be reached day or night, I was invincible.

Several times during those first two years of his life, my own mother would try to give me advice. It was all the wrong advice, of course. Few of her ideas corresponded with my infallible pediatrician.

When Mark was about two years old, we moved to another state. About six months later our little girl, Leah, arrived. Mother came to spend two weeks with us while I convalesced. I wanted everything to be as congenial as it could be during her visit, but I knew I had a horrible attitude about almost everything Mother told me.

Things went very well for Mother while I was in the

hospital. The day I came home, however, things changed. Mother, remembering my old attitude, came under a pressure to do everything the way I wanted it done. "Where do I put this?" she would ask. "How should I cook the chicken? Do you let Mark do that? Should I let him go there?"

It soon became apparent to me that Mother too had been aware of my critical, disapproving attitude. "Mother," I said, "you did all those things the way you wanted to do them when I was in the hospital. Please keep on doing them that way. Do things the way you would if you were at home."

"But, I want to do everything the way *you* would do them," Mother protested.

"That's silly. You have been doing these things for years." Then surprising myself I added, "I could probably learn some things from you."

Those two weeks became joyous and meaningful as Mother and I began to relax and enjoy one another. We prayed together, cried together, worked together. I came to realize that my mother was a wellspring of good advice and information. I liked the calm way she handled Mark, and envied her assurance and peace when she bathed little Leah.

She knew more about raising children than I could imagine. The fact that she had successfully mothered three children had never occurred to me before.

Those weeks together taught me a lesson I have cherished and used for many years now. If our hearts and ears are open to hear, we may find many others have shared the same frustrations and fears.

Good advice can come from many places, even your own mother.

4

Chapter 3
Kitty and the Mockingbird

Kitty, a small tabby cat, spent the summer at our house. Our vacationing neighbors had asked us to feed her.

The only problem we had with Kitty was her entourage. Wherever she went a company of noisy, yapping birds followed her. They pecked at her nose, tail, ear. The mockingbird was definitely the leader of the bird pack. She did not seem to have a nest to care for. Even though it was summer and all respectable birds were staying close to their nests and new babies, she would follow Kitty for blocks picking and pecking.

Kitty did not seem to mind the birds. It seemed almost as if she was playing along with them. She would sit very still letting the birds get closer and more bold each day.

One morning the cat was not accompanied by the usual squawks of the mockingbird. The next day we found the bird on my neighbor's doorstep in five pieces. "I guess

Kitty finally got tired of that pesky bird," the children commented.

Solomon gave us some good advice. "Don't be conceited, sure of your own wisdom. Instead, trust and reverence the Lord and turn your back on evil; when you do that, then you will be given renewed health and vitality" (Pro. 3: 7,8).

How many times have I been like that mockingbird. Sometimes, I'm not content to stay in the nest, or nitch God has given me. Part of my job as a mother is to resist the devil, but very often I go chasing him into situations I have no business being involved in. Instead of staying home where I belong, I become convinced God can't possibly run His Kingdom without my finger in every pie.

The devil doesn't mind at all if I pester him. Why he allows me to pick, peck and squawk. He is content for me to be bold and clever.

Too often I have almost ended up like the mockingbird. Sometimes in order to teach me a lesson God has allowed the devil to come very close to pulling me apart. Sure it is always the devil that does the pulling but my own conceit is my real downfall.

If the mockingbird had continued to care for her nest, she would have stayed out of trouble. Likewise, when I stay in my place, I can and will avoid much heartache and trouble.

Trusting God in my little nitch can be difficult. Turning my back to evil even harder. But, Solomon promised that when we trust God and turn our backs on evil we are given new health and vitality.

Believe me, with three children and a husband to take care of, that is exactly what I need.

Chapter 4
Who's Afraid of a Three-Year-Old?

My good friend, Wylene, tells of the panic she experienced after reading the chapter in Dr. Spock's, *Baby and Child Care,* on making an infant formula. She memorized the chapter but was convinced she would never be able to make that mystical recipe. Necessity, of course, meant that she would have to make it. After two or three times of getting in there and making the needed formula, she was amazed at how easy it all was. "I can't imagine now why I was so terrified," she laughingly says.

In an interesting article by Dr. Spock, he was lamenting the fact that many parents have become terrified with the idea of raising their children. He said he was beginning to feel too many parents were looking to textbooks and child psychology books for answers which should come from within. He said there are many things that we will

7

just naturally do right if we don't know any better. After all, parents have been raising their children for thousands of years without textbooks, his included.

I am always amazed by mothers who give their children the impression that they are afraid of them. One day I was keeping a particularly rambunctious three-year-old. I told him to pick up his toys. When he refused, I took his hand in mine. His hand guided by mine started picking up the toys. This made him very angry. He came at me with both fists. I grabbed the flying little hands. I held them firmly in one of my hands and said quietly, but firmly, "Dear, I am not afraid of you. I am much bigger than you are. Not only that, I am tougher than you are too. Now you pick up those toys."

His three-year-old temper and frustration continued to flair. "You are afraid of me. My mother is afraid of me!" he yelled.

I tried to smile a controlled smile of unconcern. "Oh, no. Mother isn't afraid of you. You just think she is."

"Yes, she is." Feet and legs flailed to give emphasis to his scream.

"Well, I am definitely not afraid of you. Get those toys picked up now!"

Who's afraid of a three year old? Many mothers. They are afraid of doing the wrong thing. Fear grips and controls every action and reaction when dealing with their children.

The Bible says. "God hath not given you a spirit of fear but of love, joy and a sound mind."

One of the biggest things a mother transfers to her child is her feelings. Children respond more to your joy, love, anxieties and fears than to your words.

Am I afraid of my three-year-old or my fifteen-year-old? That fear will rob me of the kind of relationship God desires me to have with my children. I must begin today, this minute, to ask God to change that fear into a Godly confidence. The kind of confidence which says to my child, "I am not afraid of you. I'm your mother."

Chapter 5
Prayer and the Bible

The best way I can teach my child to love prayer is to pray. The best way to teach my child to love reading his Bible is to read my Bible.

Three basic things which are required for Christian growth are prayer, Bible study and Christian fellowship.

For almost all children, fellowship comes naturally. Every child wants to be around other people. Even though some children do not like to be coddled too much, they all want and need a certain amount of affection and companionship. If a child is accustomed to having fellowship with Christian friends, he will seek out that same companionship when he is an adult.

Prayer and Bible study also will come through your example. If you have not established a set time for prayer and Bible study, do it. Today is the best time to begin that discipline in your life.

Our private devotions should be the center of our lives.
When my children were smaller, naptime was my time to
be with the Lord. I would let nothing come between me
and my time of prayer. It became the mainstay for me
during those turbulent years of joy and sorrow. I remember one day when the children were very small.
Things had gone from bad to worse. I had gone out to the
laundry room where I suddenly crumpled in tears and
frustration. I sank to my knees in despair. An old chair
covered with spilt soap flakes became my altar. There
have been few times when I have been more aware of the
Lord's presence.

Now that the children are older, my need and desire
for prayer has intensified. I find after everyone is asleep I
can slip into the living room, and there study my Bible.
The house is quiet.

Just before I go to bed, I slip into each child's room,
put my hands on each of them and pray. Often they will
awaken, smile and kiss me. Most of the time they are not
even aware of my presence. As they lay there sweet and at
peace, I ask God to minister to each of their special needs.
At times when I know extra prayer is needed for one of
the children, I linger and pray in the Spirit as the Holy
Spirit does the needed work in their hearts.

Prayer time for me now is in the morning, just after I
get up. I have for years gone back to bed for thirty
minutes or so before I get the children up for school.
Now I spend that time in prayer.

Because I am a "night people" this has been especially
difficult for me. I don't even wake up until three o'clock
in the afternoon. For me to spend time in prayer before
seven o'clock was absolutely out of the question. During
those first mornings when I was getting adjusted to stay-

ing up, I would pray, "Help! Lord. I don't want to pray. Make me want to pray. All I want to do is sleep." I have found this time has become so precious I cannot imagine beginning my busy day without it.

Once Charles Wesley was asked how he could afford to take several hours out of his busy schedule to pray. He replied, "I am so busy, sir, I cannot afford not to take several hours out of my time to pray."

Charles Wesley had twenty-four hours in his day. I have twenty-four hours in my day. Charles Wesley prayed hours each day. His influence was spread around the world.

Prayer and Bible study are essential in my Christian walk. They are essential for my children, too. As I teach them about their heavenly Father, I must teach them the importance of talking to Him and having Him talk to them. The best way I can teach my children to love God's Word and talk to Him is to be sure they see the example in my life.

Chapter 6
Quiet Times

I read a Dennis the Menace cartoon once. Dennis' mother with frazzled hair and wrinkled dress was ushering him upstairs. The caption read, "I know, Dennis. You don't need a nap but I do."

How do mothers survive if their preschoolers don't take naps?

My schedule for the day goes something like this:

6:30 I get up. Thirty minutes of prayer and then *bedlam*.

12:32 (Two minutes after lunch is eaten) Naptime.

2:00 Naptime is over. More *bedlam*.

8:30 The children's bedtime.

That heavenly quiet oasis in the middle of my day is like a cool dip in a mountain stream after a hot sticky hike up the mountain. I don't always need a nap. I do always need the quiet.

Even during the summer months when the older children are home from school we all need a quiet time. They are required to come in for about an hour of quiet play. Everyone needs a break of calm relaxation to regather and revamp.

Several years ago a young mother came to a friend for advice about her three-year-old son. "I can't stand him anymore," the young mother confessed. "I never thought I would ever say that about my own son but it's true. I feel like I have to have a break from him sometime. Am I wrong for feeling like I have to have some peace and quiet?"

"Are you kidding?" her friend laughed. "You came to the wrong person if you think I'm going to tell you that you should grin and bear the pressure.

"Personally, I have wondered how you put up with it as long as you have. I really like your son. He's a good little boy, but all day is too much. Why don't you give him a nap after lunch?"

"Oh, that would never work," the young mother said throwing her hands up in the air. "I tried it. Even as a baby, he would not take naps. I don't think he has taken a nap since he was six months old. He just lays in his bed and screams."

"Well, even if he doesn't need a nap, you do. Put him to bed. Tell him that he doesn't have to go to sleep, but he must lie still and quiet. And do not let him get out of the bed. Try it and see what happens."

"Okay," the young mother said. "I'll try it. I'll try anything."

Several months passed. My friend stopped by the young mother's house one day at one o'clock. Before she could knock on the door, the mother met her and put her finger to her mouth. "Sh-h-h-h. Tommy's asleep."

They didn't discuss Tommy's naptime that day. But since then she has talked to other harassed young mothers. "Put him to bed and make him take a nap," she always advises. "Your child will be a different person when he wakes up. You will have had a break too. It's the best thing that ever happened to me, putting Tommy to bed in the afternoons."

God said, "Be still and know that I am God." It is very hard to "be still" with an eighteen-month-old hanging on you and pulling your hair.

Put him to bed. Don't let him scream or cry and don't let him get out of the bed. See what happens. He may not need the nap but you do.

Chapter 7
I Can't Wait for School to Start

For years I would sit with neighbors and friends who had older children. They lamented each summer away. They would stare glassy-eyed into space repeating, "I can't wait for school to start. I can't wait for school to start."

I would always hold my prideful shoulders a little higher. I loved having my children home. I was not at all anxious for them to start school. The first years Mark was in school I would count the days until each vacation period would start. Summer vacation was a time for real rejoicing for all of us. It was important to me to have my children safely under my wing.

After several years, I did notice my attitude begin to change. I found I liked being able to plan my day. Carol, my three-year-old, was still at home, but I could always take her with me. I had worked out a good schedule.

19

With my housework finished by nine o'clock, I would have time for sewing, needlework, reading, my piano.

Finally, last summer I came to see this whole situation from a new and different perspective. I was sitting with a friend after a haggard battle-weary week of three discontented children. I moaned, "I can't wait for school to start. Look at this house. Look at me! I can't get anything done. It isn't the children's fault totally. I'm so disorganized. All I seem to do is referee fights. Oh," I groaned, "I'll just be so glad when school starts."

Before I could become guilty about my rash and harsh statement, I saw this was a real sign of maturity.

My children are older now. They need me less. Many times they are happier when they have the discipline of school. They need to be away me sometimes. Brothers and sisters need to be away from each other. They need to be with new people, new faces, new friends.

There is no shame in wanting school to start. No. It is a sign of real maturity.

Chapter 8
I'm Too Tired To Be Spiritual

There are some things you should never confess. This is probably one of those things. I really do not like to pray with my children when they go to bed.

By the time they are bathed and ready for bed, I am too tired to be spiritual. All I really want to do is yell, "Get in the bed and go to sleep!" Yet I know that teaching children to pray before they go to sleep is vital. So we continue to have our prayer time.

In order to make it more palatable for me, we have tried many prayer techniques. We have tried Rosalind Rinker's concept of just conversing with God. That seemed to be working fine until I fell asleep one night in the middle of our conversation.

Then we tried praying with our eyes open. That didn't work either. I became distracted by the children's constant wiggling. We tried praying for a new person each night. That didn't work. I always forgot who I had prayed for the night before. I seemed to end up praying for the missionaries in Africa every night. Then Leah would have to correct me. "Mommy, you prayed for them last night."

Finally, I gave up trying to make it different or even enjoyable for me. The children enjoy this special time we have together. They either enjoy it or it means they can stay up another few minutes. I haven't decided which. All I know is they will never let me forget their nightly prayers.

As a child, I can remember the times our family prayed before going to bed. They are good, warm memories. I loved our prayer times together. Sure it meant I got to stay up those few precious minutes longer, but there was more to it than that. There was a drawing together with our heavenly Father which made our night's rest more peaceful.

That is the other reason why we have continued our nightly prayer time. I know for a fact it makes a difference in a child's life. It made a difference in mine.

Even if I do not like having to take time with my children, I will. It is important for them.

As the children have grown older, I see this prayer time has been essential for me also. I need that disciplined time of prayer with them. I need to do some things for the Lord I really don't want to do.

For each of us there are little sacrifices we must make for the growth of our children in Jesus. We don't do them because we enjoy them. We do them because we know God is faithful. We know He is a rewarder of those who diligently seek Him.

Chapter 9
My Kids Are Driving Me Crazy

When my children were five and two years old, I would often suffer from a common malady I have named crazyitis.

The symptoms of crazyitis are these. By ten o'clock in the morning, I would be so exasperated and tired my only thought would be, "My kids are driving me crazy!"

I learned there was one sure cure for crazyitis. Taking a picnic lunch, a good book and some sunglasses, we would head for the nearest beach or park. We never stayed the whole day—usually only an hour or two. But we did it often, very often.

If I could find another mother suffering from crazyitis, I would drag her along with us. They were usually easy to find. You can pick one up in most any suburban house which has a preschooler living in it.

I must admit I don't ever remember learning any deep

23

spiritual truths while at the park. Usually the children would play and I would read or talk to my friend. But I always knew when it came time to go home my crazyitis would be gone. I would be able to face those dirty dishes, unmade beds, bathtub rings and smelly toilets.

The children always thought our picnics were planned just for them. That was an added bonus. I got brownie points in motherhood. They never knew and I never told them the real reason we went. We did it only for me. It was the only absolutely sure remedy I knew of for crazyitis.

Chapter 10
Discipline and Jesus' Authority

"Why should I discipline my child? After all, he is sweet and lovable. The few things he does wrong aren't even as bad as the things that I do that are wrong." I was in the kitchen clearing up the dishes after supper as I mused about this problem of discipline.

As I scraped a plate, I remembered a word I had felt the Lord had given me several years ago. *I want you to learn to discipline your children the way I discipline you.* The message had been clear to me. The Lord was saying, *Look at the way I discipline you. Follow my example.* But Jesus never has turned me over and applied the rod of correction to my posterior.

No, the Lord spoke gently to my heart, *but I gave you parents to do it for me. By the time you were an adult, you had learned the value of punishment. You had learned a healthy respect for authority. You knew God was to be feared. Now I can bring correction in other ways.*

"Was that the value of parental discipline?" I wondered. I had often chafed just remembering the young man in the Old Testament who had been stoned because he sassed his mother. Was his sin greater than just being a smart-mouth kid? Yes, of course. He did not respect or fear the authority which was over him. He did not respect his parents. Therefore, he could not respect or fear the ultimate authority—God.

If you are a child of God's, He is going to correct and punish you. Hebrews says, "My son, despise not thou the chastening of the Lord, nor faint when thou art rebuked of him: for whom the Lord loveth he chasteneth, and scourgeth every son whom he receiveth" (Hebrews 12:5, 6). Discipline and punishment are a part of our Christian life.

God wants children who know how to receive discipline and correction. How much better for my children if God can start with a son who knows what obedience means. When God speaks to a son, He wants to be able to speak only one time. Then He wants His son to obey.

God is infinitely patient with His children but He continues to punish that child until he is able to listen and obey.

It was so clear now. "Why should I punish my child?" God is building a well-disciplined family of sons. If my children can learn at a young age to obey authority, they will be better suited to fit into God's family.

Much of the chipping and training will be finished before they become adults. They will know how to hear the voice of God. They will understand what it means to be a people who are under authority.

They will not be chafed when God, the ultimate authority of the universe, speaks and says, *Son, I want you to do an unpleasant task. I know you don't want to do it. But you will do it because I want it done.*

They will understand their position in the family of God. They will know they are sons under authority and will say, "Here I am, Lord. Send me."

Chapter 11
The Value of a Touch

I did not know hands were made to touch, caress and love my child. I did not know they were never intended to be used for correcting my children.

Psychologists have learned the value of a touch to a child. I am told that experiments were made on two sets of children. One set was held, caressed, patted and touched by their parents and others. The second set was not held or touched. They were orphans who were in a hospital ward where they could receive little or no individual attention. The difference in the mental, emotional and physical development of the children was remarkable.

Set One came out high on all the tests. Set Two came out extremely low. They had been carefully screened in these experiments. The main difference in their upbringing was the touching Set One had received.

In Proverbs, God says, "Foolishness is bound in the heart of a child; but the rod of correction shall drive it far from him" (Proverbs 22:15). Hands were never intended by God as rods of correction. When my children were little I didn't know this.

By the time Mark and Leah, my two older children, had become four or five years old, they had developed a most disconcerting habit. They ducked everytime they passed me.

I did not know why they did it, but I knew I didn't like it. One day Mark passed me and ducked. When I had finished my usual reprimand to him, I asked, "Why do you duck whenever you pass me?"

His answer was heartbreaking for me, "I'm afraid of you. I'm afraid you will hit me. If you don't hit me when I go by, you will probably pinch me or something." I knew he was telling the truth. He was not trying to be impertinent. I was guilty.

My hand had always seemed to be the most convenient thing with which to punish my children. It seemed like such a hassle to go and get a stick or the ruler to spank them.

The one definite drawback I had clearly seen to using my hand was it hurt me. Many times after I had spanked my children, I knew why some parents would say, "This is going to hurt me more than it does you." My hands would sting. Occasionally I would hit a belt buckle or a button and I would even break blood vessels in my hand. It really did hurt me more than it had them.

That day I resolved that unless there was a critical situation, I would not punish my children again by spanking them with my hands.

When we decided to adopt a puppy dog, we were told

by the humane society, "Do not punish your dog with your hand. Use a rolled up newspaper. Then the dog will be afraid of the newspaper, not your hand. Your hands should give directions and loving, not discipline." This same psychology applies to children. Children will be afraid of the object which gives them the punishment. If a switch from a tree is used, he will be afraid of the stick. Not your hand.

There were many times that it seemed my hand was the ideal thing to punish my child with, but I came to trust God's wisdom about this matter. God said use a rod. This word from the Hebrew means a small branch from a tree. It did not take long for me to see the desired result. All I had to say was "go get my stick," and tears would flow.

But the nicest result was I found my children no longer ducked when they passed me, even though I may have been very angry with them. They are no longer afraid of my hands.

Not only that, I don't have stinging hands or broken blood vessels anymore!

Chapter 12
Discipline—the Right and Wrong Way

Once a week at least, my mother would look at me with the stern, glaring eye of disapproval and say through clinched teeth, "You are begging for a spanking!" I never knew until I had children of my own what she was talking about. I was sure the last thing I wanted was a spanking. I most certainly was not about to beg for one.

After my children came to a certain age I found myself repeating my mother's words, "What you want is a spanking." My children would give me the same blank look I'm sure I must have given my mother.

I would put off the inevitable punishment until the last possible moment. I would try coaxing, coddling, screaming. Finally I would see my lovely child become an awful brat. Then I would be forced to spank him.

PRESTO! When the tears stopped and the turmoil had

33

calmed down, I was always amazed. The awful brat had disappeared into thin air and my lovely child had wonderfully reappeared as happy and sweet as ever.

It is little wonder that my children did not know what to expect from me for I was inconsistent in my discipline. I usually waited until I became desperate before I punished them.

Discipline is never easy for the child or the mother. Consistency in applying the discipline is the only thing which will cut down on the number of times a child must be disciplined. A child trained to obey the first time will obey the first time.

About four years ago we began our program of consistency with our children's discipline. The first two weeks were hard, very hard. I had to spank my children so many times a day I expected their little behinds to be bruised. "How can I go the rest of my life, doing this? It's going to take more discipline on my part than I have," I honestly confessed to myself. Yet I felt that for my children's Christian growth, I must be consistent. Then after about three weeks a wonderful thing happened. After that initial hard training period, I found I was having to spank my children fewer and fewer times a day. In fact, I was amazed. When I spoke (not screamed, just spoke) to them they obeyed.

Consistency is the key. Jesus is very consistent with my training. He never gives up. He is always after me—leading me into paths of righteousness. With His help, I can train my children. They will learn what to expect from me. Therefore, they will be happier and healthier children because of it.

Chapter 13
Correct What Bugs You the Most

Paul was two years old when his parents came to know Jesus as their Savior. It was a drastic, revolutionary change for the whole family.

Paul's mother had always felt a child should not be disciplined at all. His father had gone along with her feelings. She believed any kind of reprimand would somehow stunt him mentally and emotionally. At two years of age with no discipline, Paul was an unhappy, extremely active little fellow.

A few weeks after becoming Christians, Paul's parents came to understand Paul must have some discipline. It had been a hard decision for them to make, especially for his mother.

When she first heard that Christians spank their children, she was horrified. "Never!" she thought. "I will never be so brutal." She decided she would write a book on the "proper" way to discipline a child. She would use the Bible as her point of reference. She began to study. She looked up every Scripture passage she could find on children or parents. After several hours of study, she gave up.

Raising her hands in surrender, she prayed, "All right, Lord. I see from the Bible that I am supposed to discipline my child. I see that the scriptural way is to spank him. I give in."

Paul's mother and father prayed together. Once their decision was made that the scriptural way to discipline was to spank, they decided to go the full gamut. It would not matter how small the infractions were. If Paul did something wrong, he would be punished.

After two weeks of constant spankings, Paul's mother was a wreck. She was exhausted from the strain. Also she felt if she had to look at Paul's bottom one more time she would scream.

She really got desperate. Yes, she could see a big difference in Paul. He had already begun to settle down. But she felt she could not take another day, another minute, of the tension which had filled her life these past two weeks. To go from no discipline at all to punishing every little thing was just too much for her.

In her desperation she prayed, "Help!" Almost immediately she knew what she should do. She would correct those things that bugged her the most.

She had tried to correct everything. The least infraction of the house rules had meant a spanking. For a child who had never known any kind of discipline, it had become almost cruel.

She quickly made up a mental list. "I will not allow Paul

to pitch a fit. I won't allow him to hit me or scream at me or his father. He cannot go into the refrigerator for food between meals." She listed all the things which she knew had to be changed immediately. Other things she would let slide and correct them later. She would allow him to take off his shoes outside. She would allow him to pull the dog's tail as long as the dog was not being hurt.

She made her list the length she felt she could handle. Then she set to work with renewed enthusiasm to help Paul into a more disciplined, enjoyable childhood.

Before two months had passed, Paul knew what to expect from mother should he try to scream or pitch a fit. The screaming had stopped. In fact most of the things on his mother's mental list had almost disappeared. Paul's mother added several new things to her list. "It's time for Paul to stop pulling the dog's tail."

She found that weekly she was adding new disciplines.

Paul became a new child. Within six months, her friends were commenting on his new behavior. They were amazed at how much he had grown up. He had become a happy little boy.

Paul's mother had learned from the Master Teacher a time-worn trick of the teaching profession. Begin your correction with the things that disturb you the most.

When my son, Mark, went into the fifth grade his teacher was a strict disciplinarian. One day when we were talking she confided, "I know Mark thinks I am really putting the pressure on him. Actually there are so many things I am letting slide for the time being. I won't let them slide all year however. We will have to deal with them later. By the time he has completed fifth grade, we will have dealt with most of his bad study habits."

When God picks us for his heavenly family, there are a

multitude of bad habits and undisciplined areas in our lives. We become new creatures in Jesus, but much of the old fleshly life hangs on.

God takes our lifetime to work on them. He doesn't insist that we become perfect overnight. He begins to work on only a few of our undisciplined areas. Once we have learned the lessons he wants to teach us about those dark spots, His loving light exposes new areas of darkness.

Too often mothers become discouraged when they first begin to correctly discipline their children because they are trying to correct everything. Most children did not get in their undisciplined state overnight. It will take several months to really begin to get a foothold in many areas. Take Paul's mother's advice, "Correct what bugs you the most."

Leave the rest until later. With the Lord, there is time. There is all eternity.

Chapter 14
Why Tell Her to Stop?

Leah and I had been visiting a neighbor's house. Leah was about eighteen months old and into everything. She had touched something she knew was off limits. I spanked her hands until she began to cry. Then after about fifteen seconds of weeping and wailing, I said to her, "That's enough. Stop crying."

My neighbor put her hands on her hips and said, "You always spank your children until they cry. Then you tell them to stop crying. Why do you do that?"

"I don't know." I shrugged in all honesty.

"My father used to do that to us too," my neighbor said. "It really bothers me. I think it is most unfair. I think you should let the child cry."

When I thought about it, it did seem unfair. Why did I make the children stop crying after I had spanked them? I knew why I wanted them to cry. Tears have a cleansing, healing effect. They show a repentant nature. Yes, I wanted the children to cry but why did I want them to stop?

After that conversation, I sensed that perhaps I had been unfair. So, I decided I would no longer make them stop crying. They could cry their little hearts out if they wanted to.

That was a mistake. After about two years I came to realize how grave a mistake it had been. Leah could not control herself or her crying. Her unrestrained crying had soon deteriorated into screaming. Screaming deteriorated into pitching little fits.

For a long time I could not imagine what I was doing wrong. Mark, the older child, was spanked, cried a little, then stopped. Leah went into crying tantrums.

One day as I had my quiet time with the Lord, I saw the problem. Mark had been required to stop crying at a young age. By the time I had decided to quit making him stop, stopping was a set pattern in his young life. He could control himself. He had been taught to control his own spirit.

Leah, on the other hand, had been allowed to cry and cry and cry. She had never been taught how to control herself.

In Proverbs 16:32 it says, "He that ruleth his spirit is better than he that taketh a city."

I knew the damage I had done to Leah was repairable. She would learn to control herself. What would have taken only months to teach her at a young impressionable age; however, has taken several years.

Many times she had to get double and triple punishments. One spanking would be for what she did wrong.

40

Then she would have to be spanked again for running away from the punishment.

It was a terrible struggle for her and for me. Then one day, before a spanking, I could see a change in her. She became determined to take her punishment the right way. She gritted her teeth, and held her arms by her sides. She was determined she would be in control.

After her punishment, I held and kissed her. I knew a victory had been won in her young life.

She has learned this lesson well. She learned to rule her spirit. Now when punishment has to be given, she will usually lay down and take it just like the Proverbs man would have.

Why do you tell your children to stop crying? "He that ruleth his spirit is better than he that taketh a city." All children are like Leah. They need to control their spirits.

Chapter 15
Pierced Ears Aren't a Sin

Denise had wanted pierced ears for years. She had begged, pleaded, coaxed and cried. Denise's mother had remained adamantly against pierced ears until the day Denise became thirteen when she decided to allow her to have her heart's desire.

Denise's mother had given in but what difference did it really make? Pierced ears aren't a sin.

We all have our own little pet peeves. For each of us there are things we have vowed our children will not do. Usually those are the very things our children want to do.

An understanding mother becomes like a willow. She learns to bend and turn with the breeze. There are many things God intends for us to remain adamantly against. Those things can be lumped into a large category called *sin*. We should never give our children permission to do

43

things which in our hearts or from the Scriptures we know are sin.

Yet there are many things that we just don't want our children to do. I know a mother who believed little girls should not be allowed to play in the dirt. (Dirt is very dirty, you know.)

Unfortunately, or maybe fortunately, she had two little girls who loved to play in the dirt. She fought this dirty problem for several years. Finally she came to realize she had been wrong. Her girls wanted to play in the dirt and it really was not a sin. She gave in.

For her it was a compromise. A wise mother will learn to make compromises. She will never compromise with sin. Sin is wrong and always will be wrong. She will learn to compromise with her pet peeves.

In a practical way you are saying, "I respect you and your wishes." The value of these compromises will be found in the times when you must put your foot down to things that are wrong in your child's life. Even though it probably will never be put into words your child will sense in his spirit, "Mother really feels this is sin. She knows this is wrong. After all I know she's fair with me. She did give in when I wanted to have my ears pierced."

Paul had learned the value of compromise. In First Corinthians 10:33 he said, "Even as I please all men in all things not seeking mine own profit but the profit of the many, that they may be saved."

You may even be like Denise's mother. Last winter she went out and had her own ears pierced!

Chapter 16
Two Make an Argument

Everyone's attention had turned to Jackie Buckingham. We had had a teaching on children. The discussion had turned to arguments we have with our children, particularly teenagers.

Jackie lives with four teenagers and a twelve-year-old. That qualifies her as an expert any day. Several people had given their opinions on how to stop arguments. Then her clear, deep voice had spoken from the front row. Without raising her head, Jackie said, "It takes two to make an argument. Just make up your mind that you will not argue with the child. There will be no argument."

I knew from past experience the value of turning to a small child and sternly saying, "I don't argue with a three-year-old," then walking off. But this was a new thought. As my children approached their teenage years, I had fallen into the trap of most mothers. Arguing. It

45

seemed so easy to take the opposite side, especially when I knew I was right.

A scene I remembered from being in the Buckingham home flashed through my mind. One of the teenagers had come in all fired up to go to the beach. "Can I go, Mom?"

Jackie looked her sibling squarely in the eye and said a calm "No."

The teenager continued to explain in eloquent terms why he must go to the beach. He concluded his remarks with, "So can I go?"

Jackie had continued with her job and did not even look up. "Well, Mom, can I go? P-p-please!"

Looking up only slightly as she reached for another towel to fold, Jackie said quietly, "I said no and I will not change my mind."

The teenage monologue continued for several minutes. Unmoved, Jackie heard him out. Eventually he left. There had been no argument. She had heard him out but she had stuck to her quiet "No" position.

I knew that for Jackie this was more than theory. She had presented a practical, working principle. She had spoken with the authority of someone who knew from experience what she was talking about.

I was excited. Could this work with my arguing eleven-year-old? When he burst home from school he had the rest of his day planned. "Mom, can I go to Steven's? We are going to clean out his hamster cage."

"No," I replied firmly. "Your room smells like a hamster cage. Go and clean it."

"But, Mom, I have already told Steven I would be there." On and on he explained why he must go to Steven's.

46

I looked at him. I tried to show the same stern but loving authority I have seen Jackie show her son. I said, "No. Now clean your room. I won't argue."

Mark headed out the door toward his room. "Can I go to Steven's *after* I clean my room?"

"Of course," I said as a grin spread across my stern face of authority.

It worked! There had been no argument.

I could not help but giggle a relieved, "Thank you, Lord."

I still fall back into the trap of arguing with my children. But I soon grow weary of the battle and remember Jackie's quiet voice, "It takes two to make an argument. If you refuse to argue, there will be no argument."

Chapter 17
Watch Your Confession

Kenneth Hagin once said, "I have good children because I confess good children."

He was speaking on the importance of our confession as Christians. I had been aware of the Scripture in Revelation, "And they overcame by the word of their testimony and the blood of the Lamb." Yet I had never thought of applying it to my children's lives.

I thought it was cute to say, "Oh, Leah, you are such a bad girl." I did not really mean she was bad. It was for me a term of affection. I wanted to say something to her but I was embarrassed to brag on her.

When Mark was only a baby, I had gone to visit a neighbor. Mark was playing good naturedly on the floor. I reached down and picked him up. I wanted to squeeze him and say, "You are such a good boy," but I was afraid my neighbor would think I was bragging. So I said instead, "Oh, you are such a bad little boy."

My neighbor sensed the harmful impact of my thoughtless words. "Linda," she said to me, "you really don't think he is bad, do you?"

"No, of course not," I said surprised at her frankness.

"Then why did you say it? Don't ever say children are bad." She paused for a few moments staring out the window. Then she continued, "Even if they are bad, don't say it. Just last weekend we had a family visiting us. Their little six-year-old boy is bad, really bad. His mother makes the situation worse by telling him all the time that he is bad and mean. I'm convinced that most of his problem comes from the fact that his mother tells him how bad he is.

"It really hurts me to hear you say that to my little Markie," she lovingly reached for him. She held him in her arms and gently rocked him, "Even if you don't really mean it."

I knew she was right. Yet I did not put her advice into practice until years later when I saw in the Bible that our confession is the way we overcome the world. I was appalled.

I had been confessing bad children for years.

That day as I listened to Kenneth Hagin teach, I saw the importance of my words. What a heavy weight they carry.

We are told that no word is lost. Even the rocks and walls act like giant recorders. The vibrations of our voices set motion patterns in their molecules which are a permanent, sealed record of each word we speak.

After pondering the importance of my confessions, I quietly repented. "Lord, I have made a terrible mistake with Mark and Leah," I said. "Help me, Lord. Teach me how to confess to You and the universe that I have good children."

In the years which have followed I have found my confession is vital to the well being of my children. They will perform up to my expectations. My confidence in them will carry them through many temptations and trials.

I will never forget one day when I was a senior in high school. I had an ideal chance to cheat on a test I had not studied for. During an exam I was called out of the room. Without any chance of being caught, I could have gone to my locker, looked in my book and gotten the answers.

One thing stopped me. My mother. I knew she was proud of the fact that I was known as an honest girl. There was no doubt she would be prouder of me if I failed the test and did not cheat than if I cheated and made one hundred per cent.

Though I was a Christian and loved the Lord, God was still a figure in the sky. He was not real or tangible. My mother's love and confidence were tangible. She was real. Her love was real.

I didn't cheat on the test. I didn't because I knew the confidence my mother had placed in me.

I am still learning how important our confession is in our Christian lives. How important it is to our children. Each day I renew my dependence on the Lord for only He can teach me. He can show me how to use my words to improve and enlighten my children.

Chapter 18
The Way of Love

Beverly's eyes brimmed with tears. Our conversation had begun lightly enough. But, all of a sudden, we'd touched a painful subject.

"People don't seem to like Bobby," she confided in me. Bobby was Bev's fiesty, slightly rebellious five-year-old. "I'm sure part of the problem is my fault. I really have a hard time correcting him. I can hardly resist hugging him even when he's bad."

Bobby bombed into the house about that time screaming, "Give me a drink of water!"

"Don't run, dear," Bev said in a small voice as she obediently went to the cabinet for a glass. Bobby made two more death-defying turns around the kitchen and headed for the family room. He picked up a vase.

"Put that down. I have told you many times not to touch that vase." Bobby slammed it onto the table.

"I don't blame people for their attitude, I guess. He is overbearing at times but he's only a child."

Beverly laughed as Bobby drained the glass of water, kissed her with a wet mouth and headed outside again.

The tears were gone.

I could understand Beverly's concern for her child. I had gone through a similar blow several years ago. A close friend had let me know that she didn't like one of our children. I had been hurt and stunned.

Graciously, however, the Lord had lead me to share my problem with an older Christian woman.

"What can I do?" I asked this more experienced mother.

"When I was younger," my friend began, "I learned that being lenient with my children is not the way of love."

Her statement struck a strong cord of truth with me. I had allowed my little ones to get by with too much only to find that others were not as tolerant as I. Yet, I wanted my children to be liked and accepted.

As a mother, it has often been hard to be objective about my children. Oh, I can see most of their faults and shortcomings, but I love them. Mothers have this capacity for love and understanding with their offspring. Others are not always as kind.

Later that day, I shared with Beverly the good advice I had been given. Together we looked through the Scriptures. We found that the Bible says Jesus grew in wisdom and favor with God and man.

Everyone wants to be liked by others. Children are no exception. Even though it is usually the mother who is the first to be hurt when others reject her children.

Sometimes even a teenager doesn't know how to act or

respond in order to make other people like them. It is our job and responsibility as mothers to mold them. Show them how to behave, how to be accepted.

"I think I'll write that motto down and put it on my mirror," Beverly said as I left. "Being lenient is not the way of love."

Chapter 19
I'm a New Person

For years I practiced "on again, off again" discipline. When I got very angry at the children, I would discipline them severely. When I felt bad, they were made to walk a straight line.

I depended on my feelings to control how much or how little discipline they received. Even though I was more strict than some parents, I was ruled by my emotions.

I screamed a lot, I kept myself in a constant state of upheaval. All that screaming made my adrenal glands work overtime. You could never call me a calm or serene person. I screamed too much. I lost my temper continually.

When I discovered the concept of consistent discipline, it made a new person out of me. Actually it took me about two weeks to realize what was happening. One day I realized I was no longer reacting to my children. I did not wait to get angry before I disciplined them. Discipline was beginning to really pay off and make sense.

I was seeing a difference all right. The biggest difference was in me.

The children did not wait to see my evil eye before they obeyed. They did not wait to hear my screeching scream. When I told them to do something, they did it. It was simple. The main difference I saw in them was they were learning to obey immediately.

The difference in me, however, was phenomenal. I could not believe how much calmer I had become. Most of my reasons for losing my temper had disappeared. I did not have to vent my anger in order for the children to obey. They were learning to obey when I spoke in a calm voice.

A friend told me recently about her former neighbor. Her name was Jessie. "Jessie was a real gem," my friend shared. "She never let circumstances control her temperament. If the children spilt the milk, she would get up and clean the mess. She would not scream or reprimand. Over and over Jessie exhibited this calm, collected sense of peace."

Finally one day my friend went to Jessie and said, "I have to know how you do it. You always seem to be in control. You let everything slide right over your head. I have been observing you for several years now, and I know this is no act. You have an aura about you that is different. What is it?"

Jessie smiled, "Well, I'm not sure. But I will tell you one thing. When I got married and the first of the children came along, I asked the Lord to do something in my heart. I knew I could not go out and earn a part of the living. I knew my place was here with the children. I asked God to make me the center of peace in our home. I began to practice that peace. It isn't always easy with five children. Yet God helped me to keep in mind my important place as peacemaker."

Jesus said in Matthew 5:9, "Blessed are the peacemakers for they shall be called the sons of God."

As important as a disciplined life is for my children, the main changes have not been in their lives. Change has come into my life. I now see my role not as a strict, screaming mother but as a peacemaker.

Children and husbands face a hard tough world. They deserve to come home to a mother or a wife who is not a nag or a screamer. They need someone who is in control. They need a haven of peace.

Havens of peace are made not conceived. They are made by peacemakers. Peacemakers who are like Jessie and all other mothers who take their jobs seriously.

Chapter 20
Dunk Mama

We have a summer tradition at our house. It's a game the children and I play called Dunk Mama. It all started several years ago very much by accident.

We were playing in our backyard swimming pool when one of the children asked, "Could I dunk you?"

"Only if you can," I replied pushing him under the water. We are all good swimmers. We understand the rules of water safety. Under ordinary circumstances, dunking is not allowed. But soon everyone was engaged in mortal combat. I was the target.

It was a lovely time. After that it became an unspoken tradition that each time I went into the pool, Dunk Mama would begin.

All through the years we have had one hard and fast rule. Frank and I are the children's parents. We aren't their friends. Friends are special but you can have many, many friends. There is only one spot in your heart for a mother or father though.

We felt it was best not to allow the children to play with us or talk to us as they would a friend. We have tried to keep our relationships in proper perspective.

But Dunk Mama is the exception in our house. There are no holds barred in that game. In fact, I'm the intended victim. I've heard all my life that exceptions only prove the rule. Our dunking game has proven our "mother is not a friend" rule.

A mother with four children came in from outside one afternoon. She was huffing and puffing. A tall, lanky woman, she had played basketball in school. Now she played with her children. She is a firm subscriber to the "mother-not-a-friend" rule but basketball is her exception. She is good at basketball. She wants her children to play hard. And they do.

"They can almost beat me," she puffed that day in her soft southern drawl.

Children need to know their parents aren't friends. They need to have the special relationship a child can have only with a mother and father. But children need Dunk Mama games and basketball, too. They need the exception that proves the rule.

Chapter 21
God Gives the Parent Authority

Several years ago I became involved with a young child who had demonic problems. Her situation was much like many of the children who are described in the Bible. Her mother and father did not believe in demon possession.

Without the mother's permission a friend and I took this little girl to a preacher who had successfully prayed for many people who were demon possessed. Nothing happened. He would not pray for the little girl. "When the girl's mother or father decide she must have deliverance, she can be helped." The preacher shared with us as we stood on his front porch getting ready to leave.

I knew in my heart he had said the right thing. I had not seen the authority of the parent in spiritual matters until that night.

In the Scriptures each time a child was healed or delivered, he was brought to Jesus by a parent. Sometimes it was a mother. Sometimes it was a father. Not one child came to Jesus for healing on his own. Every one was brought.

Over and over testimonies are given of praying mothers or fathers who prayed one rebellious child after another into God's Kingdom. Many times the child is involved in unbelievable sin. Drugs. Sex. Violence. Yet the authority God has given a parent for his child is even more unbelievable.

Many psychologists and ministers have said there is no such thing as a problem child. There are only problem parents. Authority and responsibility always go hand in hand. Jesus said, "To whom much is given much is expected." Each parent is given a life. A blob of clay life is placed into our hands. God says in essence, "They are your responsibility. I have given you the authority." God has given us the greatest responsibility of the universe, another life.

But He knows we are not faithful. Yet where we are faithless, He is faithful. If a parent will seek Him, He will take up where we leave off.

Recently we heard a young woman share her experiences. No matter how far she strayed away from the Lord and salvation, her mother was there. She was there praying, encouraging, loving.

It seemed from the young woman's side of the story the mother had done no wrong. But I think it would be interesting to hear the mother's side. If you talked to the mother, I'm sure she would have shared another part of the picture. We could have seen a side of discouragement, sometimes fear, many times failure.

Then the young woman told of an experience her

mother had which ultimately had changed their lives. Three years before the daughter had come to the Lord, God planted faith in this mother's heart. She was given faith to turn her daughter completely over to God. One day in prayer she said, "Lord, you can do anything you have to do. Just bring my daughter back to you. I take my hands off." Things went from bad to worse as this young woman sought everything. Finally after three years, the daughter turned her heart over to Jesus.

Authority means responsibility. God has given the authority of our children to us. It is an awesome responsibility. It is a responsibility no mere human can handle. Each of us must come even as this mother did and say to God, "Lord, I turn my child over to You. You take her. Do anything You have to. Just bring her back to You. I take my hands off."

Then and only then can God fully take control. Then He can place in our hearts faith that will never fail, love that is all kind, all compassion, all forgiving. Encouragement that will sustain even the hardest heart.

God has given the parent the authority over his child. Overwhelming responsibility? Yes, oh, yes. Far too much for us to handle. We must turn our children over to Him. For He is faithful. Jesus. He will never, never, never fail.

Chapter 22
Presenting a United Front

I've always been impressed with my sister's self-control. In all the times our families have been together, I never heard her interfere with the punishment her husband would give their sons.

I found it impossible not to side with our children when Frank would correct them. I try to be firm with them and I appreciate Frank's firmness. Yet my protective mother instinct would rise in full force whenever Frank would even fuss with them. I could always find excuses for them.

One afternoon while my sister's family was visiting in our home, my brother-in-law had to punish one of his boys. My sister and I sat at the table. "How do you do it, Ferne? I have never seen you interfere with any correction Billy has given the boys. I can never stay out of it. I always see the children's side of the issue when Frank is trying to correct them. I always take their side. This is one area I cannot seem to get any victory in. I know it is important to present a united front. I don't want to undermine Frank's authority. I want the children to know I'm backing him, but I can't seem to stay out of it."

Ferne laughed as she sat with her hands folded and resting on the table. "You grit your teeth and clench your fists!" she said. "Actually," she straightened her dress, still smiling, "You aren't the only one who has that problem. It's almost impossible for me too. But I have just made up my mind I won't interfere. So I don't."

"You mean to tell me it's just that simple. You just make up your mind not to and you don't."

"Well, Linda, I had to pray about it a lot. But when the boys were small I determined with the Lord's help I would not interfere with Billy's disciplining of the children. And I don't."

I'm not sure what I had wanted her to say, but that was definitely not it. I wanted her to give me some tricky one, two, three solution. Some magic phrase to repeat. A super spiritual prayer to pray. "That's it?" I asked her again.

"That's it."

"Okay," I determined. "I'll try it. I'll stop looking for the easy way out. I know it has worked for you. It can work for me."

The acid test came the same afternoon. Leah was the culprit. She did something which she knew was wrong and had to be punished. I silently prayed, "Lord, help me keep quiet." Then I bit my lip. It worked.

Presenting a united front is important to children. It is very difficult for most mothers. However, with the Lord's help and endurance we can do it.

68

Chapter 23
Rebellion in My Heart

Several months passed after my sister and her family's visit. Each time I was tempted to interfere with one of Frank's disciplinary decisions, I would pray and bite my lip. It was not easy. I could still see the children's position, and I had a sore lip.

After I had taken those first halting steps though, God showed me a disturbing thing about my attitude. I saw the reason it was hard for me to quit interfering. There was rebellion in my heart. I did not accept my husband's place as final authority in our home.

In all honesty I felt I was better equipped and knew more about disciplining the children. Therefore, I thought I should be the one who had the last say about how they were disciplined.

God showed me this was rebellion. Only it was not

rebellion toward Frank. I was rebelling against God. Frank had not placed himself as the head of our home. God had. If I preferred another arrangement, it was rebellion against God.

I did not like the attitudes which had been cropping up in me. It seemed fine to question Frank, but God was making it clear to me, I was not questioning him. I was questioning God. I knew my rebellious questioning was sin.

Sin in a Christian calls for repentance. It took the Lord several months to even get me to the place where I wanted to repent. I wanted to hang onto my rebellion just in case Frank might make some drastic mistakes somewhere along the line and I would have to take over the authority.

Even though I can't pinpoint the time or place, I did change my mind about Frank's place in our home. One day I became aware of a new attitude in me. I somehow knew God had not made a mistake. Frank was the head of our home and he would have the final say. I wondered how I could have wanted it the other way around. How could I have ever wanted such awesome responsibility. I was not equipped emotionally or physically to handle that important a task.

The rebellion in my heart melted away as I accepted once and for all Frank's position of authority. As I submitted to God through Frank, I found it easier and easier to back him in his measures of discipline.

It became natural to esteem him before his children. I have often wondered to myself, "How could I have been so blind? Why couldn't I see the wisdom Frank uses in dealing with them? How have I missed his gentleness and humor?"

I had been obviously blinded by my own self worth and conceit. My blindness had even covered an obvious sin in my life. Rebellion. It was only after I decided to do something about the conceit, that God began to reveal and deal with the rebellion in my heart.

Chapter 24
Learning to Unlapse

One day after a short bout with the flu and three days cooped up in the house, I found three-year-old Mark curled up hidden behind a large chair. "What in the world are you doing back there?" I asked him.

Mark looked up at me with wide eyes. "I just had to go somewhere to 'unlapse' and be by myself."

Even as young children, most of us realize our need for privacy. Somewhere in our quest to be good mothers though, we occasionally forget this one essential part of being a whole person.

We forget privacy—a time to be by ourselves, alone.

When I was a young girl, I shared a bedroom with my sister, so, there was not a special room that was designated as mine. There were few places that I could go to be alone. But I found a secluded little patch of smooth

73

green grass between the house and a fence, and I would curl up in there with my solitude.

As a mother, I have had to learn to set aside certain times to be alone. These are never large blocks of time. I need only a few minutes. Sometimes I'll take an afternoon stroll around the block. I reserve the time it takes to change my clothes for me. The few minutes I spend in the bathroom are mine. No matter how short these periods are, they have become moments just for me. During these small retreats from my children, I am simply myself. I enjoy my own company.

Jesus instructed us to "Love our neighbors as we love ourselves." He was saying that I am to love myself. For I cannot love others until I love myself. But often we don't love ourselves—we become so busy and involved we don't even know who we are or our place in God's plan. I must take some time out to be by myself.

We all need our privacy. We all need a special time when we can "unlapse" and be by ourselves.

Chapter 25
Have Time with Your Husband

When Mark, my first child was only two or three weeks old, my mother sat me down on the couch.

"Honey," she said, "If you don't take any other advice I give you, listen to this. Remember, don't become so wrapped up in your children's lives that you forget you and your husband have a life too.

"You have to have a life of your own. In about twenty years your children will be gone. You will still have twenty or thirty years to live without them with your husband. Don't become so out of touch with yourself and your husband you don't know each other when the children have to leave home.

"We found there was only one way to have time to ourselves when the children were young. Get the kids to bed early in the evening. Don't let them stay awake to all hours. You must have some time with your husband.

"Remember, when you were living at home, your bedtime was always early."

I did remember that. Even while I was in high school, bedtime was nine-thirty. We did not always have to go to sleep, but we did have to be in our rooms.

"Well," mother continued, "I did that on purpose. I always put you children to bed early so that your daddy and I could have some time to ourselves. You need time with your husband."

I remembered friends of ours with small children who did not go to bed until eleven or twelve o'clock at night. The children went to bed when the parents did. I had not thought about it before, but our friends did not have any time to be together and alone.

I did not want that to happen to Frank and me.

I sensed it was important to maintain a link with my husband. I knew that would take time. Time alone.

I put Mark to bed early that night. Since then, all three children have gone to bed early. Even when daylight savings time was put in effect in our state, and they had to go to bed in the daylight, our rule remained firm.

Our times together have made us happier, more united. We have not lost touch with each other. We have had time to iron out differences. Sometimes the ironing was painful and loud but we have had the time alone and together.

In those days I did not always take the advice my mother would pass on to me. I knew, however, mother was speaking from her experience. She had always shared her life with my father. He had shared his life with her. I also knew that in recent years she was counseling more and more women. Often they had not remembered this vital ingredient in marriage.

Just a few months ago a friend of mine echoed these same words, "Don't make the mistake my husband and I made. We became so involved in raising our children, we lost touch with each other. Fortunately for us it isn't too late. But we lost so many years we could have been companions for one another. I'm afraid we were just parents for our children."

While visiting the nursing home one day, I came upon an old man. I had seen him there many times. He was in the hall leading to the office, struggling to wheel his chair toward the office door.

"Can I help you?" I asked. "Can I push you somewhere?"

"No," he said with a toothless smile. "I'm going to the office to call my wife. I was supposed to sing for the church service tonight. The service has been called off. I don't want her to have to make the trip down here for nothing."

He paused. Then with a big grin he gave his wife the nicest compliment a husband can give, "She's my best friend, you know," he said. "We were friends before we fell in love and got married. She is still my best friend." We both smiled as he made his way toward the office.

Children are a blessing from the Lord but they are not to be a substitute for a life of your own.

Chapter 26
Snoopy, the Nicest Thing We Ever Knew

Snoopy's grave stone is a wooden piece of board. The inscription is painted in dripping red paint. It reads, "Snoopy, the nicest thing we ever knew."

Snoopy had become a part of our family only five weeks before. He was an adorable, dachshund puppy. His long floppy ears and short quick legs soon had the run of the whole house.

It had been a turbulent five weeks to say the least. He was not house trained and I was soon beside myself with the cleaning and scrubbing trying to eliminate the odor. But I had loved him at first sight and that love had grown over the weeks.

I had promised a neighbor I would go to a nearby city to visit her daughter in the hospital. I made plans to go and asked a friend to go with me.

When I put Snoopy outside that morning, I was glad it

was a sunny day. I did not want to leave him inside to mess in the house for the whole day. I was not concerned about the swimming pool. He had never ventured near the water. All of our neighbors who had pools had never had any accidents with their pets. So I was sure nothing would happen.

I got back from my trip late in the afternoon. It had started to rain about 10 o'clock in the morning, and had rained all day. As I got out of the car, several children ran up to the car. Their faces were flushed with excitement. "Snoopy's dead! Snoopy's dead!" they yelled. "He drowned in the pool!"

I was shocked. It had seemed that the Lord had given Snoopy to us. Now this. I ran to "Miss Betty's" house across the street. Mark and Leah were there. They were shaken and shaking. Mark had found Snoopy at the bottom of the pool and had gone in to get him. I was not home and they had needed someone. They had taken Snoopy to "Miss Betty's."

I carried the children and lifeless Snoopy home. Mark began to dig his grave and make his tombstone. I was so crushed and broken I called Frank at work. "Snoopy's dead. He drowned while I was in Orlando."

Frank's response shook me. "You had to go to Orlando, didn't you? If you had been home, this would not have happened." He was not angry. There was no sarcasm or criticism in his voice. He was stating a fact. I did not want to hear that kind of correction. "Frank," I said through my tears, "I can't listen to that. I have to go."

Supper was a bitter-sweet mixture of tears and laughter as we remembered all the silly little things Snoopy would do. After supper, Frank stayed at the table. "Linda, I have to talk to you."

This time I knew I had to listen. "Linda, you always have time for everyone else. What about your own family. I know you don't neglect us, but what about all the little things you do for others? You seldom do them for us. God allowed this terrible thing to happen to help you see something. I'm not angry with you, but there are some things that you must learn about loving your family."

I sat at the table crushed. I knew God had spoken to me through my husband. He had not wanted to say those things but they were needed and he was right.

It was true. I so often got caught up in being the ideal church woman that my children and family suffered. As I sat at the table, my heart began to cry out to God, "Lord, I don't want to hear what Frank has said to me. I want to justify and make excuses. But, Oh, God, he is right!"

I saw the monumental responsibility God had placed on my shoulders as a wife and mother. It could not be taken lightly.

Skimming the surface would not do. I had to do more than what was required of me. I understood for the first time what Jesus had meant in the parable he told about servants. He said when the servants come in from a day's work in the fields they don't expect to sit down to a hot meal.

No. They have to then prepare the meal for their master. Jesus said when you have done only those things which are required of you, you must consider yourself an unprofitable servant.

I had always seen this as a hard demanding task. Now I could see it in a different light. I wanted to be the one to comfort and love my children in their times of sorrow. I had not been home to fix Mark and Leah hot chocolate.

"Miss Betty" had washed Mark's face and wrapped him in a warm blanket.

Sure, I was a good mother, but an unprofitable one.

God did a new work in my heart that day as I lingered at the dinner table. I felt no condemnation or even self pity. I only resolved anew that I would become God's profitable servant.

God had given Snoopy to me. I would learn the lesson God was trying to teach me. I knew it would not be easy, but my Father is longsuffering. He can show me how to begin to do the added little extras that will make me a profitable servant.

Chapter 27
I'm Mean. Pray for Me

I understand most poisonous snakes are mean. They will attack any warm-blooded creature in their path. Their eyesight is not very good, yet they can sense heat coming from a body and will attack the warmth.

I am sometimes that way also. I am just plain snake-in-the-grass mean. Although I have seen the time when I enjoyed being "Villain for the Day," I usually don't even like myself when I act that mean.

Like the snake, I will attack any warm-blooded thing that crosses my path, especially vulnerable little creatures like children.

One day, when I was at my meanest, I got sick and tired of myself. Mark and Leah were the only ones who were around. Suddenly, I knew I had to have prayer. Then I felt I would be all right. I sat Leah and Mark down and said, "Listen, you two, I have a problem. I'm mean."

They shook their heads in agreement, "We know, Mom."

"Well, I need prayer. Will you pray for me? I don't want to act this way. I have tried to do better but I can't. Please pray for me."

Four tender hands reached out to touch me. Mark prayed first, "Lord, thank you for my mommy and help her not to be mean anymore."

We had to stop for a minute so I could explain why I was crying before Leah prayed.

The change was wonderful. I was completely transformed.

Each time I have submitted in this same way to their simple prayers, I have been changed.

It is always humbling for me to ask for their prayers. It is even more humbling to admit I am being mean. But they have never been harsh or unforgiving.

The Bible speaks of the time when a little child will lead a lion and a snake. For me, that part of the kingdom has already come. For I have had four tender little hands touch my hurting bleeding spirit and pray, "Lord, please help my mommy."

Chapter 28
I'm Sorry

Gwen had company for the night. The young guest had never been in Gwen's home before. The two girls were allowed to sleep downstairs so they could have privacy. They also wanted to be able to talk after the rest of the family had gone to bed.

Gwen's parents had to get up at six o'clock in the morning. When one o'clock came, the girls were still giggling and talking. Gwen's mother came downstairs and told the girls to stop talking and get to bed. At 2:30 Gwen's father came downstairs and told the girls to stop talking and get to sleep. At four o'clock Gwen's mother came downstairs. She was angry.

She yelled at the girls. "Your father has to get up and go to work at six o'clock! March up those stairs and go into Gwen's room both of you. Now *go to sleep!*"

Gwen's mother crawled into bed again. The house was at last quiet but she could not sleep. There was another voice keeping her awake. This one did not come from Gwen's bedroom. It was a still small Voice from within her spirit. "You were wrong," the silent Voice insisted. "They were wrong but you were wrong too. Now you go and apologize to those girls."

Gwen's mother fought that tiny Voice for several minutes. Finally at four-thirty she could struggle no more. She got up and gently knocked on Gwen's bedroom door. "Girls, I'm sorry. I shouldn't have yelled. I shouldn't have been angry. You were wrong to talk until so late but I was wrong too. I want you to forgive me."

Gwen's mother knows the importance of telling children openly and honestly, "I am sorry. I was wrong."

A neighbor once told me, "Never admit to your children you were wrong about anything. They will lose respect for you if you do."

I have found just the opposite to be true. Your children know when you are being unfair. Usually they know it before you do. They do not want a little tin goddess who can admit no wrong. They want a flesh and blood person who can hug them close and say, "I was wrong. I am sorry. Please forgive me."

Chapter 29
Children Need Privacy

Children need privacy. Beginning at an early age they must be allowed to have time alone. There are several ways we have learned to help our children have their privacy.

First, we don't insist our children share all of their toys. We let each child have one special toy which he doesn't have to share. For our little girls, it's usually a dolly. Mark always had a truck or GI Joe which was his special toy.

Another thing we learned quite by accident. One Christmas, when Mark was two years old, he received two identical riding horses. We thought about exchanging one of them but we never did get around to it. We found this horse soon became his favorite toy. It was the one toy he never felt he had to share. He had a duplicate which could be shared with a friend. Each one of the children at one time or another have gotten identical gifts. Each time this toy became their favorite. None of the toys were expensive. The reason they were their favorite was obvious. They could be a little selfish and still share with a friend.

Times alone are essential too. Even small children need times to be by themselves.

Every mother knows that when the house gets quiet it is time to check. Their child is usually into something they should not be. Many times though by hastily yelling for my child I have interrupted a special time of privacy. Once that time is broken, somehow it can never be regained.

I learned if possible to go and look for the child instead of calling for him. If he is into something he shouldn't be, I have caught him red-handed. However, if he is only having a private time, I do not interrupt his play.

As an older child, I found my needs for privacy became greater. My parents were adding several rooms to our house during one summer. They were putting a large walk-in closet at the end of one of the rooms. It seems I spent one whole summer in that closet with the door closed. Mostly I was reading. My mother never asked what I was doing in there. She had enough wisdom to allow me to have my privacy.

Closed bedroom doors usually mean, "Please knock before you come in." That applies to mothers too.

One mother had become so accustomed to walking in the bathroom while her son was in there that when he became a teenager she continued doing it. One day he came to her. "Mother," he said, "Daddy doesn't come in the bathroom when my sister is taking her bath. Please don't walk in on me."

The mother was shocked at her own lack of consideration and behavior. Her son was right, of course. He had every right to his privacy even from his mother.

As each child develops, he will require different ways for a mother to show him she respects him as an individual. Allowing times of privacy will become one of the keys. It is a concrete way she can say to her child, "You are my child but you are a unique individual. You need time to learn about yourself. You need sometime to be by yourself. You need your privacy."

Chapter 30
I'll Take a Bored Baby Everytime

My first reaction was to come under condemnation. I had just finished reading a very informative newspaper article about babies. The article had been relating some new information just gathered about babies who sleep a lot. Because all three of my children had been good sleepers, I was interested.

The article reported the findings of scientists who had been studying sleep patterns of infants and small children. These eminent scientists said that in times past it was thought that babies who took several naps a day were good babies. These new studies had proven they were not good babies. They were just bored. They had not been properly stimulated to keep them awake, therefore they preferred to sleep.

The article continued to relate other new and exciting

facts. The fact that babies who sleep a lot seem to be happier, better natured babies probably stemmed from their added excitement when their boredom was broken.

The scientists conducting the tests were not sure what effects boredom would have on the child as he developed. But there was a clear indication from the article that the effects were most certainly bad.

After my initial reaction, I came to my senses. My three boredom sufferers had developed into happy healthy youngsters. The effects could not have been too severe. Then I began to laugh at myself. "I'll take a bored baby any day," I thought. As I remembered those tired years, my smile grew. "Their boredom was probably the only thing that kept me and them sane."

"Remember how you used to get tired just watching them run around," I consoled myself. "I wonder what would've happened had they been properly stimulated."

Babies are dynamic little bundles of energy. They move and wiggle more in one minute that we do in one hour. That movement is necessary for proper growth, but it is also very tiring.

Babies who sleep regularly may be bored but they sure are more fun.

Chapter 31
Let the Kid Cry

I am always amazed by mothers who ask, "What should I do about my child? Each time I put him in his crib or playpen he cries."

The answer is so simple I almost choke it out, "Let the kid cry."

When our third child was born, the older children were ten and six years old. It was like living with two grandparents. They could not stand to see her cry even for one second. They felt something must be dreadfully wrong if she even whimpered. When it came time for little Carol, to learn to stay in the playpen, it was summer vacation time. The older children were home all day. I would put Carol in the playpen. She would immediately begin to cry and they would take her out.

I could not get it through their heads they were not doing Carol a favor by taking her out of the playpen just because she was crying.

Even though they learned they must not take her out, they did not like it. They would stand at the playpen and try to soothe her and play with her. This, of course, only made matters worse. They were sure I was the cruelest mother in the world.

By the time they had been in school one week, Carol had adjusted to the playpen. She did not cry anymore. She played happily.

One day they came in from school. There was Carol in her playpen happy as a lark. "How did you do it Mom?" they asked. "Carol isn't crying at all. She even likes it. Look at her she's playing and happy. How did you do it?"

"Easy," I said as I folded diapers. "I did what I had been telling you two to do. I ignored her and let her cry. She learned after a few days she was not going to get any sympathy from me. She stopped crying and started to enjoy herself."

Cribs and playpens are probably the most wonderful inventions for mothers. During that first hectic year, babies are more mobile than they should be. They can get into too many things in our modern homes that can harm and even kill them. For their own protection, they should be confined.

No child is going to like that confinement at first. He will balk, scream and holler. It isn't easy, but if you can let them cry, they will learn you are not going to take them out. Eventually they will become interested in a toy. Before you know what has happened, they will be playing—happy to have a place that is theirs.

Then you can rest. If you should have to make a quick trip out of the room, your child is safe. Playpens are probably the safest places you can put your children.

In the end, it does pay to let him cry. In his playpen there are no electric cords, no hot irons, no unnoticed poisons. There are only toys, padding and safety.

Chapter 32
Snakes, Squirrels, and Manatee

A beautiful garter snake hung by its tail from the tree about twenty feet from our campsite. A small crowd soon gathered to see the graceful ballet as it danced to the music of the swishing leaves. The two younger girls squealed and jumped in frightened glee. Mark, their braver, older brother stood and watched the snake with a fascinated eye.

Mark took great pains to teach three-year-old Carol later that afternoon. She wondered why the squirrels were constantly gathering food. We had watched these energetic little rodents all day. They picked up every bit of food we would throw to them. Then they would run up the trees to their nests. They became so brave after an hour or so that we had to chase them away from our supplies.

Each time we left our campsite for even a minute, they would descend on the picnic table looking for crumbs and other goodies.

"The squirrels don't eat all the food they take to their nests." Mark stooped down to speak right into Carol's face. He talked clearly and simply making sure she understood what he was saying. "Most of it they store until winter time. That way they will have food for the winter. They will have something to eat and they won't die."

After supper we took a walk down to the clear, blue springs. There in the water were two manatee. We all wanted to jump in the stream for a ride on their huge backs.

Manatee are large water mammals. Many of them live in the larger rivers here in Florida. They are susceptible to pneumonia though and stay in the warmer waters of the smaller streams during the winter. The manatee are friendly with man and seem to delight in his company. They are quite playful and like to carry people on their backs.

That night I lay in our tent unable to fall asleep. As I contemplated the day's events I saw once again that children need snakes, squirrels and manatee. They need to know about the wonderful world God has made and given to us. They need to know why God made the world and the important part they play in God's plan.

Each experience can and should become a time to teach our children about their heavenly Father. Children, always ready and eager to learn, are like empty, priceless vessels waiting to be filled. What a responsibility we have to see that these vessels are filled with equally priceless treasures, like snakes, squirrels and manatee.

Chapter 33
Don't Correct Other People's Children

When my children were much smaller, I thought God had placed me here on the earth to correct all the spoiled children in creation. If someone came to my house with a child who misbehaved, I took it upon myself to tell the child and his mother how he should behave. I became the self-appointed mother of the world. I must admit I found this a tremendous burden to bear. Yet I really did not realize the load I had taken was self-appointed until one day I was talking to my friend Danya.

Danya has two girls. They are the same ages as my older children. Danya is perhaps the strictest disciplinarian I have ever known. As a consequence her girls were extremely well-behaved.

We were just chit-chatting when she said, "You know, I used to think I could help mothers who did not know how to handle their children by telling them all the things they were doing wrong. I also used to try to correct other people's children. I was so bold I would correct them in front of their parents. I found I lost a lot of friends that way.

"Recently," she continued, "I asked God to help me keep my mouth shut and mind my own business. I try to never correct other people's children now. Since then the strangest thing has happened. People are coming to me for advice. They want to know what I did to have such good girls.

"It's become almost amusing. I find myself putting them off. The more I try to stall though, the more they want to know about how I discipline the girls."

She paused for a moment while she brushed back her long, brown hair. Then she made this observation, "People sure are funny when it comes to their children."

"Oh, my, what a slap in the face." I thought back quickly. "Had I ever tried to correct her girls?" No. I was sure I hadn't. I couldn't even remember seeing them do anything wrong. I breathed a sigh of relief. I was sure she had not been talking to me. I was glad when the conversation turned to another subject.

We continued to talk but my mind would not stay on the subject. It was racing away, "Danya couldn't be getting in a sideways slur," I thought. "I'm sure she isn't trying to tell me in an off hand way to stop correcting her girls. Then why do I feel so guilty?"

All my thoughts came to a screaming halt. A quiet small Voice spoke from somewhere inside my heart, "Linda, I'm speaking to you." I did not have to ask who it was speaking. I knew it was the Lord. "It's time you learned the lesson Danya has learned. Mind your own business.

You aren't the world's greatest mother. You don't have all the answers. Stop acting like you do."

I knew then the Lord had spoken to me through my friend Danya. That is probably the most valuable piece of sideways advice I ever received. Now I wonder how I could have been so stupid.

Other people should be given the leeway to raise their own children. Each person will expect something different from his child. In Hebrews 12:10 we read, "For they (our earthly fathers) chastened us after their own pleasure." None of us know the complete mind and heart of God when it comes to raising our children. We all discipline our children the way we think is best.

Paul said, "Don't be conceited and overestimate your own value" (Romans 12:16 Amp.).

None of us have the complete answer on how to correctly raise a child. We all fail miserably. But in our failures we do learn.

I have probably learned more from my failures than from my successes. Others will also learn from their failures. Even though I still "overestimate my own value" many times and would like to be the mother of the world again, God usually stops me.

Once I come back to my senses I'm always glad. For Danya was right about another thing. People are funny when it comes to their children.

Chapter 34
I'd Never Spank Someone Else's Child

I had just spanked Timothy. We were keeping him for a
few days while his parents were out of town. He had
bitten our two-year-old several times. This morning he
had pulled a handful of hair out of her head. When I saw
the matted hair clutched in his chubby fist, I knew he
would have to be disciplined with a spanking.

After about an hour I saw the humor in the situation.
Once again a child had made me do the very thing I had
boasted I would never do.

One week before, I had made a final statement of fact.
"I would never spank someone else's child." I boasted.
That boast wasn't bad enough. I added fuel to my fire of
pride and said, "With other people's children, I can always find some other way to handle the situation!"

What is it about these exuberant packages of energy,

love and original sin? They unwittingly but invariably turn all our sound resolutions into just so many words.

I wonder if God has given us children to teach us that without Him we can do nothing. Jesus will never fail. But we do, especially when a child is around. It seems almost like God is interested in breaking down those things we are most adamantly determined to hold on to. In that way, He can step in and gently say, "Do you need some help? I can help you. I have the answer for you."

As I turn in my weakness and desperation to Him, I find He not only has the answer, He is the answer. Sometimes it's nice to fail in my boastful resolutions just so I can see anew who is my real source of help.

Chapter 35
Kids Would Demolish the World in a Week

Dee and I sat in a busy hamburger joint having lunch. We were enjoying our talk about the party she had had at her house several days before. The boys at the party ranged in age from three to twelve. The action and games had gotten more and more fierce. Finally one of the boys had been hurt and we had to break everything up.

Dee laughed as she munched her hamburger. "You know if it weren't for parents, kids would demolish the world in a week!" She emphasized her statement with a brisk wipe of her mouth with her napkin.

I could not help but remember all the times my mother would say to us, "Stop before someone gets hurt." Of course, we never did stop and someone always ended up hurt.

My children don't stop either.

My third grade teacher used to say to us, "If I give you an inch you take a country mile." I never understood what she was talking about when I was a child. Now that I have children of my own, I know exactly what she meant.

Part of the charm of a child is they know no bounds. Their love, compassion, faith and virtue seem endless.

Yet, as well as being one of their greatest assets, it is also probably their biggest downfall. Children need and want limits put on them. They need someone who cares enough to say, "You will not do that, and if you do, you will be in trouble with me."

My sister and I used to sleep in the same double bed when we were growing up. She would draw an imaginary line down the center of the bed and say, "You cannot cross over this line. If you do, I will clobber you. This is my side of the bed. You can't come over here." I would delight in pushing my finger as close to the center of the bed as I could. I would not cross her line however. I knew she really would hit me.

As parents, we all draw imaginary lines. Some of us draw a fair and consistent line. We say don't cross this line or you will be in trouble. Some of us change the line from day to day. Some days we will give them the whole bed. Other days we give them less than half. We leave our children confused. They must be continually pushing us. They are always trying to find out where the line is for today.

As we finished our hamburgers and left the restaurant, our two little ones ran for the playground. "Don't run! Walk!" Dee called to her son. He stopped running and started to walk across the pavement.

Dee had drawn an imaginary line. Her son did not know it but she had done it for his own good. He probably assumed the line had been drawn just so he could not run. Dee had known the dangers of running on the pavement, however. She did not want him to fall and hurt himself or someone else.

"It's true," I thought to myself as I crossed the parking lot to the playground trailing my three-year-old. "Without parents kids would demolish the world."

The children were already in the playground running, pushing, falling. "Yep," I thought, "and they would be sure that they were only having fun."

Chapter 36
We Prayed or We Didn't Go

Mrs. Mary Stevens was in her eighties when she came to teach our small Bible study group. Her quiet dignity and mature judgment were a refreshing change from the fiery newly Spirit-filled Christian teachers, I had been sitting under.

One day she was teaching on prayer. She fixed her stern, solemn eyes on each of us. "Do you pray with your children before they go to school?" she asked. "As a child, if we didn't pray, we didn't go. It did not matter to mother how late we were. We prayed before we left the house each day."

Mark was in his first year at school. Those first months had been marked by a big hassle. It seemed impossible for me to get him up and out of the house without a big fight each day.

I knew the Lord was speaking to me. Prayer would make a difference.

The next morning, I got Mark up a little earlier. "Mark," I said to him, "we are going to pray this morning that Jesus will go with you. I am going to pray and I want you to pray, too."

"Okay, Mommy," Mark replied with an absent-minded smile.

I prayed a short prayer. Then he prayed. As he walked out the door, I shouted a cheery, "God bless you."

Mark ran back to kiss me again, "God bless you, too, Mommy."

The change was remarkable. We had had time, extra time. Mark had not left with my usual, "You forgot to make your bed, just wait 'till you get home," yell. He left with prayer, a smile and a kiss.

Each day since then before the children leave for school, we pray. Sometimes that prayer is prayed as we hurry for school in the car because we are running late but mostly there is more time than is needed.

When the children got old enough to read, we added a short devotional to our morning routine. They read ten verses aloud from their big print Bibles. Then we have our prayer time.

Even on the mornings when I have gotten aggravated and begun my screaming act, the children have never left with me screaming, for the Lord always touches my heart during our prayer time.

Prayer does make a difference. For us it is the difference between the hassle and haggle of last minute details turned into a cheery, "God bless you," as the children leave for school.

Chapter 37
God Will Untie the Apron Strings

My teen-age years were not easy for my mother. There were three teenagers living at home. At least once a week, mother would throw up her hands and say, "I will be so glad when you get married." Sometimes she would be talking to me, sometimes to my brother or sister.

This never made us doubt her love for us. We knew she was just being honest. It was absolutely true. She would be glad when we got married.

God was beginning to untie her apron strings. When a new born babe comes into the world, his mother cannot keep her hands off of him. When the baby cries, she is right by his side. If he doesn't cry, she's right there worried something has gone wrong. She checks at least ten times a day, just to be sure he is still breathing.

As that child matures and grows, his need for a protective mother lessens. He needs space to explore, roam. He needs to find out who he is. God has provided a wonderful love potion in all mothers. You want your children to be less dependent on you the older they become.

When our third child was born, Leah was five years old. It was a big adjustment for her. She reverted to old baby ways and habits. She was overly protective of little Carol. She would cling to me and demand the kind of attention that I had long ago stopped giving her. Now I did not have the time or desire to do all the things she was trying to demand of me.

For several months I found myself under terrible condemnation. "Don't you love Leah anymore?" I was continually chiding myself. "Don't you realize she needs your love too? Can't you allow her to act like a baby just for a few months? She will grow up soon enough." I would make up my mind I was not going to react harshly to Leah's smothering love. Then when she would begin her baby act, I would get angry all over again.

I finally got desperate enough to admit my awful reactions to a friend. Her advice was just what I needed. "Leah is not a baby anymore," she counseled me. "You should not feel guilty when you do not want her to act like one."

I remembered my mother who honestly admitted to us, "I will be so happy when you get married." Just as God was preparing my mother to enjoy the years when she did not have the responsibility of raising a family anymore, God was preparing me. It was time for Leah to begin to grow up.

Many times we chastise ourselves for feelings which God has put in our hearts. It would not be normal for a mother of a fifteen-year-old to check him during the night to make sure he is still breathing. Neither would it be normal for a mother of a one year old to be waiting for the day when her daughter would get married. God gives us special desires for special times in the lives of our children.

I pray that when I feel that first twinge of, "Oh, I wish you were grown," that I won't fight it but realize God is beginning to do a divine cutting job on my apron strings.

Chapter 38
Please, Mommy, Don't Make Me

Mark had been thrilled when I had first asked him to go into the store for me. "I'll drive you up there but I want you to go in. Go to the bread counter and get a loaf of bread," I instructed him. "Then go to the lady at the check-out counter, give her the money for the bread. She will put it in a bag and you can leave."

As we approached the store a strange silence came over Mark. When I looked at him, I could tell he was near tears. "Mommy," he finally said. "I changed my mind. I don't want to go in the store. I can't do all those things." His eyes scanned his shoes while he talked.

"Of course, you can dear, I'll tell you again what to do." Slowly I repeated the instructions.

As we pulled up to the store, Mark began to cry. "Mommy, I can't. Please, don't make me do it. Don't make me go in the store by myself."

I felt like I was sending him to the guillotine instead of the store. I really did not know what to do for a few minutes. I had always known he was going to be rather shy but this was ridiculous. He was falling apart. I quickly began to sort the facts in my head. "He was five almost six. Next September he would be going to kindergarten. He was old enough to go into the store and buy a loaf of bread.

"Mark," I said as firmly as I could. "You must learn to do new things. I know this will be different, something new, but something new is not always bad. You will be glad you went in the store after you are out. Now, I don't want another word from you. You must go in that store and get the bread."

I practically pushed my baby out of the car. I watched as he struggled to pull open the heavy entrance door to the store. The clerk saw him huffing and puffing and immediately came to his rescue. She gave me an icy stare as she let him in the big door. That settled it. I had been wrong. I should not have let him go in alone.

In a few seconds the door opened again as he pushed his way out. I couldn't believe my eyes. He was smiling. He did not have any trouble with the door coming out. As he got back in the car, I saw a new air of confidence in him. "That really wasn't so hard, Mom," he said in his deepest voice.

"Good," I started the car trying to hide my pride. Mark was growing up. He would not always want to accept the additional responsibility growth would mean for him. Sometimes he would not want to take those extra steps. Maybe he would even have to be pushed.

I thought about the mother bird who carefully takes her baby out of the nest and then drops him. At first he struggles and falls. His mother must swoop down again and again to save him. Finally he learns to spread his wings and fly.

Most baby birds do not want to leave the nest. They have to be pushed. Pushing is hard. But the pride of the baby bird who takes his first soaring flight is worth all the effort. Mother birds continue to push their fledglings out of the nest. They continue to let them drop through the air but they never let them fall.

Each time I have had to push one of my baby birds out of the nest I have remembered Mark's first experience at the store. I don't always remember his cry or his fright but I always remember that new air of confidence. I remember him saying in his deepest voice, "That really wasn't so bad, Mom."

Chapter 39
Where Did He Get That From

"I would like to know what your daughter, Leah, has done to my son!" The short, Spanish mother had fire in her eyes as she stood in front of me. "My son never bit anyone until you people came to this church. Now he bites all the time!"

I stood there with my mouth open. Her son did indeed bite. Two-year-old Leah had come home bearing his teeth marks more than once, but as far as I knew Leah had never bitten anyone. Even though I tried to explain this to the woman, she could not seem to hear. She repeated her biting statement and huffed away.

As amazed as I was, I couldn't really blame this angry mother. It is terribly hard for us mothers to realize sometimes that our little darlin' didn't escape receiving his share of the Adamic nature.

When Mark was a baby and began to show these awful character traits, I began to isolate him from his friends, one by one. "I'm sure that little girl who has been coming over here has taught him to do that!" I would explode to Frank. "I just won't let her come over here again."

Before long, he was living in my protective mother-made embryo. Then, lo and behold, new stigmas began to show up. I had quite undone myself. For I had no one to blame his bad conduct on but myself and him.

Finally, like the dawn of morning, I realized that he wasn't learning these awful things from anyone. He was born with them.

Once I had made that pride-exploding discovery, we could begin to deal with his problems. Up until that time I was so sure everyone else was to blame that we had not done much to help Mark overcome his bad character traits.

It really is the typical thing to blame someone else for bad conduct rather than get to the root of the problem. Adam was the first buck-passer. After being caught in sin, Adam's explanation was, "The woman you gave me . . ." Eve blamed the serpent.

Only as we admit our sin and shortcomings can they be dealt with. In our children this is also true. As long as we continue our biting statements and pass the buck, our children won't be helped. Their problems won't be dealt with. When we honestly and openly admit that even though they are precious and loving, they are not perfect, then our children can begin to receive help.

Chapter 40
Brothers and Sisters

Mark and Leah squabble and fight most of the time. Leah sings all the songs that irritate Mark the most. Mark knows just how to *almost* hit Leah. He comes close enough to scare her but not close enough to actually touch her.

You can't imagine my surprise several weeks ago when I found out Mark had intervened in Leah's behalf at school. We were to meet Frank at a restaurant after work. He had been detained, so for almost an hour, we talked.

It was one of those rare times when everyone was happy and laughing. Mark began telling a story about a bully who had tried to hurt Leah. Mark rode up on his bicycle just in time. Like the mounted patrol, he jumped off his bicycle yelling, "That's my sister! You had better leave her alone!"

The story fascinated me. I put my hands on my hips

and asked, "Why would you care if someone were trying to hurt her? You delight in hitting her at times."

"Mo-ther," he said in exasperation, "she is my sister!"

Who can understand that mystical bond between brother and sister? Sure they squabble and fight but love keeps them joined. When love seems to fail it is just the fact that they are brother and sister that binds them into a part of the family.

In teaching one afternoon, I mentioned that I can remember our home as a child as a haven of peace. My mother was listening to the teaching. After class she laughed, "I can't remember it as a haven of peace. I would get so upset about the arguments and confusion. I felt I was an utter failure during those hectic times."

Even though my mother and father were not aware of the peace, joy and love that permeated the children, it was there. It drew us together and made us a family of love.

I don't understand the mystical bond that joins people and makes them truly a family. Because we are human, mingled with our love for one another will be squabbles, fights and bickering. Yet the supernatural love of Jesus always seems to get through our children's hearts. That's when they start yelling, "That's my sister! You leave her alone!"

Chapter 41
Protection!

The tears streamed down Mason's fat, rosy cheeks. "Mommy, tell David to play with me. He's the only 'brodder' I got, you know. Please make him play with me."

Mason's mother wiped his tears away. "What a picture of health he is," I thought to myself as I looked at this tender mother and son scene. Elaine spoke softly, "Okay, you find David. I'll tell him to play with you."

Elaine Batson and I were sharing a Saturday afternoon while our husbands were working on the new church building. Our attention had turned to Mason. Satisfied his mother would rectify the situation, his two chubby legs ran off.

Few people would guess Mason is diabetic. Yet Mason has become the object of God's special protection. His parents have learned to walk with the Psalmist who said, "God shall cover thee with his feathers, and under his wings shalt thou trust" (Psalm 91:4).

Before we knew it Elaine was telling me Mason's story. I would like to share it just the way she did:

Mason was nineteen months old when I noticed a radical change in his behavior. He was constantly pulling and tugging at me. He gulped down water, three or four glasses at a time. I had begun to toilet train him but found I had to stop. All of that liquid flowed continually. He had lost a lot of weight. Because I was with him all the time, I had not recognized this warning signal.

He slept off and on all during the day. He would stop right in the middle of play and fall asleep.

It was a Saturday when I first realized something was really wrong. Mason could not walk. He would weave and stumble like a drunk man. "I'm going to take Mason to the doctor first thing Monday morning," I told Dave, my husband. "Something is wrong."

Dave went to church Sunday morning. I stayed home with the boys. Mason was worse. He slept almost all day.

That afternoon Dave told me to go to church at night. He offered to stay with the boys.

"No," I told him. "I want to be here." Then because God had begun showing his protection to Mason, I changed my mind. Yes. I would go to church. I did not know it but God had someone at church he wanted me to talk with.

I arrived at church early and settled in a pew.

Mrs. Bernice Manuel was seated in front of me. She turned. "How are the boys, Elaine?"

"David's fine but Mason is sick. I'm taking him to the doctor Monday. He has been acting strangely for weeks." I described Mason's condition, the weaving, drinking, sleeping.

Concern was written on her face. "Elaine," Mrs. Manuel said in a solemn voice, "I don't want to frighten you but that sounds like infantile diabetes."

I knew Mrs. Manuel's son was diabetic, but I had never discussed it with her. I knew almost nothing about the peculiarities of the disease.

"You must check Mason's urine immediately," Mrs. Manuel continued. "He could go into diabetic coma."

Dave's sister had died only a few months before. She had been diabetic. I knew a diabetic coma was serious.

Mrs. Manuel got up. "Let's go. Now! I have the equipment at home. We can check Mason's urine ourselves."

The urine analysis was simple, short and conclusive. Mason's urine showed acetones (a poison) and high sugar.

We rushed him to the emergency room. Mason's diabetic treatment was begun immediately.

The doctor explained that infantile diabetes is much more serious than diabetes in an adult. Adult diabetes can usually be treated by controlling the diet. With infantile diabetes, there is always damage to the pancreas. Mason's pancreas was not even functioning. They told me if he had gone to sleep that night, he would have gone into a diabetic coma.

125

Then because he would have been left all night, there would have been brain damage and he possibly could have died.

Great care must be taken with him. Every scratch, especially in the legs or feet, could become gangrenous. No blister or cut could be left untreated.

I left my baby in the hospital. Curly headed, blond, little Mason. It was more than I could bear. I was scared. Fear gripped my heart so hard I could hardly breathe.

How could I provide Mason with the constant, efficient care he had to have. I had always been a nervous person. As a teenager, I had taken tranquilizers.

I slipped down beside my bed. Only God could share this deep piercing hurt. I poured out my heart to Him. Tears flowed. In the middle of my grief a thought was planted into my heart. "Elaine, isn't this nice. I've chosen your son to use for awhile. Everthing is going to be okay." Suddenly, a wonderful peace settled over me. Never before had God spoken to me in this way.

I got up; all my tears were gone. The telephone rang. It was my sister. She had gotten the news from my mother. I found myself comforting her, "God has spoken to me. Everything is going to be okay."

I had a beautiful night's sleep. The next morning at the hospital, we began our training to take care of Mason. We had to learn how to give him shots. There were special diets; weighing food. What to do when insulin gets low—what to do when insulin becomes high. Coma. Shock.

My mind was clear and my nerves calm. Only a few

hours before, learning to give shots by injecting oranges or grapefruit would have put me into a state of shock. Now I had complete peace.

Mason came home after six days in the hospital. He had always been a jolly, even tempered child. Now with the strain of severe hunger and thirst as his body became adjusted, he became very cross and irritable. More and more we saw our sweet cooperative child acting like a little tyrant. We came to realize that this was not Mason.

Sometimes the pressure would almost become too much for me. The insulin shots tore at my nerves. Before you give insulin injections, you must get all air bubbles out of the syringes. Injecting air into the veins could cause death. Those first weeks I could not seem to get the air out. One day I realized God had to be in control of this situation, too. I took the authority of Jesus' name. Out loud I said, "In Jesus name I command Satan to get away from this needle and this situation." From that day on, I have had no problems getting air out of the syringe.

There were several crises. When for some reason the insulin becomes too high in the body, the diabetic must have food. Orange juice has a natural high sugar count. It is always given to avert diabetic shock.

One day Mason and I had gone for a ride on my bicycle. We had stopped and he had played. When we came home he had gone to sleep. Little David was watching television. Suddenly he called out, "Mommy, you better come to Mason. He's crying and shaking all over."

I ran for Mason. Orange juice! I had not made it up that morning. "Mommy, please help me!" Mason cried. I pulled the apple juice from the refrigerator. Second best, but maybe it would stop the shock. Mason was shaking so badly he could hardly swallow. I got the juice down him. He was still shaking. I poured sugar into a spoon and forced it down his throat. Still the shaking and shock intensified.

I was desperate. There were the emergency glucose bottles in the cabinet. I had read the instructions on the bottles many times. But I could not remember how to use the medication. I got the bottles down. I tried to read the instructions. My eyes would not focus.

Mason was not any better. I had to do something fast.

The bottles were marked ONE and TWO. Putting the needle in bottle ONE, I pulled the syringe open. Then I put the needle in bottle TWO. I drew out the second solution and shot it into Mason's arm. In a matter of seconds, Mason began to calm down.

I called the doctor. "You did all the right things," he said. "Don't bring him to the hospital. Everything is okay now."

When I had had time to calm down, I took the emergency bottles down again. I read the instructions. Bottle ONE contained a dry glucose. You have to put the wet solution of bottle TWO into bottle ONE. This dissolves the glucose. What I had done was inject only the dissolving solution into Mason. There had been no glucose in the injection. It had not mattered though. God's clear protection and provision had hovered over my son.

Dave and I have come to learn what trust actually means. In the night only God knows if Mason's body needs food. Each night we put Mason in God's care. We pray if he needs food God will awaken him. God has always answered our prayer.

Recently, I went into the pharmacy to buy Mason's supplies. There was a box and a large sign. "WIN FREE INSULIN FOR THE REST OF YOUR LIFE. SIGN FOR THE LUCKY DRAWING." I went over to the box. I almost signed Mason's name. Suddenly I stopped short. "Wait a minute," I said to myself. "Mason is not going to have this for the rest of his life."

I walked from the store rejoicing. God had put a fresh assurance of hope and faith in my heart. Mason won't be a diabetic all his life. In the meantime, praise God, he is watching over Mason and providing him with supernatural protection.

After Elaine had left to go home and I gathered up my things and the children, my heart was singing. God has a special plan for each of our lives. Things don't always go the way we would like, yet this exciting story had reassured me that God's protection and hand are continually on us.

Chapter 42
Matthew, a Gift from the Lord

I was five months pregnant. We had thought our family was complete. We had two children, a boy and a girl. Now I was pregnant again. As Frank and I sat with friends, we were laughing and talking about our delight in this unexpected new baby. "I can't understand it," the man said. "Frank, how can you be so happy about this new child? I know I wouldn't be thrilled if my wife suddenly got pregnant again."

"Well," Frank said, "the reason I'm so thrilled is God told me right from the start this was His special gift to us from Him. How can you be unhappy with a gift from the Lord?"

"Frank," I almost squealed in delighted glee, "did the Lord tell you that too? That is exactly what I had felt. That this baby was a gift from the Lord."

Even though I was five months pregnant, we had not shared with each other why we each had been delighted with this new baby. God had spoken to both of us that He was giving us a gift.

That month as I sat in the doctor's office I picked up a name booklet which was sitting on the table. We had selected a boy's name already, Matthew. But we did not have a girl's name yet. I leafed through the pages of girls' names. None of them satisfied me.

Beside each name was the name meaning. I began to look up the names of family members to find out the meanings. After looking up Mark and Frank, I turned to Matthew. There, to my surprise, were the words, "MATTHEW—A GIFT FROM THE LORD."

I was stunned. God was surely telling me that we were going to have a boy. A boy named Matthew. Hadn't He spoken to Frank and me that this baby was His gift to us?

On Christmas eve I woke up obviously in labor. It was three weeks early but I was not concerned. Both of our other babies had been born two or three weeks early. "This completes the picture," I smugly thought as I pulled on my nicest housecoat. "It's Christmas eve. Our Matthew will be a Christmas gift from the Lord."

At 10:55 a.m., Christmas eve, our gift from the Lord entered the world a beautiful little girl!

I had had natural childbirth and was fully awake when she was born. When the first initial shock wore off, I could see God's smile as I thought about how I had had everything planned. Now instead of a Matthew we have a Carol Christa who has been everything God promised. She is our gift from Him.

They wheeled me out of the delivery room. Carol was

snugly wrapped and put in my arms. The doctor had called Frank into the hall so I could tell him about our baby girl. As I rode down the hall to meet Frank, I decided I would try to stop outguessing God. When God gives you a Christmas gift, He knows how to make it a surprise.

Chapter 43
The Card

Debbie was a lively redhead with sparkling eyes. She had
been raised in a Christian home, and by nine years old
had become serious about wanting Jesus as her Savior.
She knew very well the procedure our church used to
receive new Christians. It was a public commitment. The
person wanting to accept Jesus would walk down the aisle
to the front of the church where the preacher stood,
waiting. They would pray together. Then the new con-
vert was seated, and filled out a simple information card.
The card was later read to the church.

One day her mother called to ask if I would watch
Debbie for an hour or two while she attended a meeting.

Anytime with Debbie was fun. Somehow I knew today
would be special. We sat at the dining room table.

"Debbie, do you know Jesus as your Savior?" I asked her.

"No," her eyes widened.

"Do you know how to receive Jesus into your heart? It's so simple. First you must realize you're a sinner. You have done many bad things. Then you must believe with your heart that Jesus died for your sin. Third, you confess Him as your Savior before other people."

Suddenly Debbie burst into sobs. "Oh, Mrs. Howard! I know all that and I want Jesus more than anything. But I don't know how to fill out that card!"

I didn't know whether to laugh or cry as I explained to her all about the card.

Children need caring adults. They need someone who will explain deep spiritual truths. They also need someone who will take the time to tell them "how to fill out the card."

Chapter 44
Hope You Like the Way I'm Raising Your Child

We all have to put up with spare children. Mrs. Green finally got fed up with having one of her neighbor's girls at her house day and night. One morning fuming inside she went to the neighbor's house to deal with the problem.

When the two women had settled in the kitchen over a cup of coffee, Mrs. Green exploded, "I came over this morning with a purpose." Then in her most sarcastic voice, "I want to make sure you approve of the way I'm raising your daughter." Mrs. Green expected the neighbor to react with anger. She could see her refusing to allow her daughter to come to the Greens' house again.

The neighbor only smiled sweetly without batting an eye and said, "Oh, yes, I think you are doing a fine job. Would you like another cup of coffee?"

As Mrs. Green found out, there is probably no real way to handle the spare child situation except adjust. Learning to like your children's friends will also help.

This hasn't always been easy for me. My first impression of some of the spares I find sprawled on our family room rug watching television has not been glowing or appreciative. But with the Lord's help, I'm beginning to revamp my thinking. We have deliberately started to include the children's friends in some of our special family activities.

In a relaxed atmosphere of love and acceptance, I find that the bratty little girl and whiny, freckle-faced boy aren't so bad after all. Even the spare children we find in our home can become a joy when the love of Jesus fills our hearts.

Chapter 45
Mission Field on Your Doorstep

The children were all watching Cartoon Capers while I prepared supper. I did not mind that there were nine or ten children in the house. They were sitting quietly watching television.

Just then Venita came in. "Look at all these lovely children!" she exclaimed. "You have a mission field on your door step. Why aren't you doing something about it?"

I took my wooden spoon out of the gravy and put both hands on my hips. "I don't have time. I have to cook supper."

"Well, take time!" was Venita's curt reply as she ushered all the children out to the garage. I watched her between stirs as she shared Jesus with them. She told them about Jesus' love just for them and that He was

139

willing to die on the cross for their sins. She explained that sin was doing bad things and Jesus wanted to forgive them for all the bad things they had done. Then she prayed a short simple prayer.

It had only taken five minutes for her to tell them about a loving heavenly Father and His Son, Jesus.

"Go back and watch television now," Venita told the children. "I have to leave." Turning to me she said, "See, that didn't take long, did it? You've been talking about wanting to lead people to Jesus. Start with the mission field God has given you."

Venita smiled and left.

She was right. I had never taken five minutes to tell my little neighbors about their heavenly Father.

Every woman with children has a private, built-in mission field. Children have a way of dragging in every stray kid from miles around.

Next time your mission field is making so much noise you are about to explode. Don't. Get out some cookies and milk and take five minutes to share with them about Jesus.

Chapter 46
Mrs. Stewart Is a Mother

Mrs. Stewart is ninety-four and has lived the past four years in a nursing home. A broken back and a heart condition have meant that she needs constant care and help.

In spite of her age, she is alert and perky. Because of her age, she is honest and never minces words.

I began visiting her about three years ago. At first I didn't know her and I felt I was fulfilling some kind of spiritual duty by my occasional visits. I soon grew to love and appreciate her honesty and humor. Her love for Jesus had made her into a warm but firm person.

During one of my afternoon visits, it suddenly dawned on me that this woman was a mother. Because she has outlived six of her seven children and because of her advanced years, I had divorced her in my thoughts from the role of a mother.

141

In a way, she had been a non-person who lived peace-
ably in this home. Now I saw her through different eyes.
She had been describing some of her earlier years when
she had been a mother with small children struggling in a
pioneer existence.

As I left the nursing home, I had a new and added
appreciation for Mrs. Stewart and all older women. I had
often chafed under their stern eye of disapproval as I had
sensed their annoyance at my three wiggle-worm children.

I slid into the car and began to pray aloud. "Lord, give
me the grace to love and appreciate these older people.
Teach me that their love for children hasn't diminished
even if their tolerance has."

The next afternoon my prayer was tested. Leah and I
were strolling around the neighborhood. We came to a
well-kept little house. "Mother," Leah pointed to the
house, "the old man who lives in this house is mean."

"What are you talking about?" I asked.

"He won't let any children walk on the sidewalk in
front of his house. He yells and screams at us. He even
called Bobby an ugly name."

"Who does he think he is?" was my first angry reaction.
"We pay taxes for these sidewalks. They belong to the
children as much as they belong to him." Before I could
voice the angry words, I remembered my earlier prayer.

I knew I would have to alter that prayer. The Lord
would have to give me tolerance and patience with my
older neighbors. I started to question in my mind what
hardships had shaped and molded this "mean old man's"
reactions and temperament. Perhaps he didn't have the
love of Jesus to soften the bumps and bruises he had

suffered. Maybe that was why his wrath erupted so easily at the children.

The Bible is full of admonitions to the younger generations to honor their elders. I had allowed what I saw coming from some of the older people I came in contact with to cloud my judgment. I had ignored God's Word. Older people should be treated with respect and honor.

The next time I visited Mrs. Stewart, I had a fresh awareness and love for her. Her life and quiet example had taught me a valuable scriptural truth. Now instead of a patient in a nursing home, she has become a personal friend. I know she can help and share with me. She understands, for she too, is a mother.

Chapter 47
Please and Thank You

Ginny's chubby, angelic face was wreathed in smiles. "Now, say thank you," Ginny's mother said to her two-year-old.

"Tank you, Mommy," Gin said as she toddled off with her cookie.

"That was beautiful," I congratulated Ginny's mom. "She is certainly polite for a two-year-old."

"Well, it has taken hours of practice and patience to get her to say those three simple words. Please and thank you. Now we're working on the other two tricky, trippers. I'm sorry."

Captain Kangaroo often tells the children who watch his show there are three magic words. They are "please" and "thank you." With these words you can get many things.

MOTHERS ARE PEOPLE, TOO

In our instant, jiffy, hurry-up world, have we forgotten these little niceties of yesterday? Like Ginny's mother, we should teach our children consideration for others.

How can we make children aware that politeness is important? First, we must realize it's a two-way street. Example is still the best teacher. A parent's politeness is noticed and followed by his children. Second, there is a price to pay. Ginny's mother said it well. It takes hours of practice and patience to get those simple words out of our children.

But the happiness these niceties add to all of our lives, child and adult, can never be measured.

Chapter 48
When All Else Fails—Pray

Juanita has done many things wrong as a mother. She is a terrible disciplinarian. She seems to know nothing about child psychology. Sometimes I even wonder how much common sense she has.

Yet what she lacks in discipline, psychology, and common sense, she makes up for in love and prayer.

One day as we sat in her kitchen sipping orange juice, one of her seven children came in from school. "Well, Pimples, how was your day?" she greeted her son. John was self-conscious about his skin problem. He had acne. Juanita then went into a long discourse about how he would never learn to wash his face. No one would ever like him. She went on to tell him that she was ashamed of him and his complexion.

I was appalled. "Juanita, should you put him down so badly? Don't you think it could make his problem worse?"

She turned for a second toward me then reached into the refrigerator for more orange juice. "I don't know. I just never thought about it. I don't think it bothers him though. I have been after him for years now. He still picks on his face. I can never get him to wash right."

The subject changed but I knew what the outcome of John would be. He could never amount to anything with the Lord. Juanita had failed. She did everything wrong.

Several years passed and we lost touch with our friends. Then one night I saw John at a meeting. After the service he hurried up to speak to me. I had noticed him earlier in the evening but I hadn't recognized him. He was seated in the front row with several other young men. He seemed to glow with the love of Jesus. He unashamedly worshiped the Lord with his head and arms raised.

"Oh, isn't Jesus wonderful?" John greeted me with a big Holy Spirit grin.

Later as I sat quietly before the Lord I saw a principle of redemption. God has woven this principle all through the Bible. Men (and mothers) are always failures. It really doesn't matter if we are big failures or little failures. God always seems to be going around picking up the pieces.

Even though it seems Juanita has done everything wrong, she knows how to pray. She spends hours and hours on her knees. She loves Jesus passionately. She knows how to pray her children into the kingdom of God.

As I remembered the shining, smiling face of John, I could only think of the prophecy in Joel. "I (the Lord) will restore to you the years that the locust hath eaten . . . You will be satisfied, and praise the name of the Lord your God, that hath dealt wondrously with you: and my people shall never be ashamed," Joel 2:25, 26.

Like Juanita we all have locusts in our lives. For many it is a lack of discipline, or a heart without understanding. We all fail but God is faithful. He knows how to repair hearts. God can take all the wrong things and make them right.

That night as I slipped down to my knees, I asked God to forgive me for being judgmental. Then I asked God to give me the prayer life and love for Jesus Juanita has.